The Secrets of
SUCCESSFUL
FINANCIAL
MANAGEMENT

About the authors

Denys Hill is a graduate of London University and an executive director of a small company which he founded in 1972. His previous career included sales, production management, industrial engineering and government service. He is currently researching into financial decision-making in small businesses.

L. E. (Ted) Rockley, whose death we acknowledge with regret, held degrees from London and Warwick Universities. He was Reader in Finance at Coventry Polytechnic and, having undertaken consultancy work in education and management development, established a reputation for a refreshing approach to problems of business management.

L. E. Rockley:
Capital Investment Decisions
Finance for the Non-Accountant
The Non-Accountant's Guide to Finance
Investment for Profitability
The Non-Accountant's Guide to the Balance Sheet
The Meaning of Balance Sheets and Company Reports
Finance for the Purchasing Executive
Public and Local Authority Finance
A Policy for Disclosure

Jointly with Denys Hill:
Security: its management and control

Books in the series

The Secrets of Successful Business Letters Clive Goodworth
The Secrets of Successful Copywriting Patrick Quinn
The Secrets of Successful Direct Response Marketing Frank Jefkins
The Secrets of Successful Hiring and Firing Clive Goodworth
The Secrets of Successful Leadership and People Management Clive Goodworth
The Secrets of Successful Low-budget Advertising Patrick Quinn
The Secrets of Successful Low-budget Exhibitions John Powell and Patrick Quinn
The Secrets of Successful PR and Image-making Tony Greener
The Secrets of Successful Sales Management Tony Adams
The Secrets of Successful Selling Tony Adams
The Secrets of Successful Speaking and Business Presentations Gordon Bell
The Secrets of Successful Staff Appraisal and Counselling Clive Goodworth

The Secrets of
SUCCESSFUL FINANCIAL MANAGEMENT

D. A. Hill and L. E. Rockley

HEINEMANN PROFESSIONAL PUBLISHING

Heinemann Professional Publishing
Halley Court, Jordan Hill, Oxford OX2 8EJ

OXFORD   LONDON   MELBOURNE   AUCKLAND   SINGAPORE
IBADAN   NAIROBI   GABORONE   KINGSTON

First published 1990

British Library Cataloguing in Publication Data
Hill, D. A.
    The secrets of successful financial management.
    1. Great Britain. Small firms. Financial management
    I. Title II. Rockley, L. E.
    658.15920941

ISBN 0 434 90758 8

Photoset by Deltatype Ltd, Ellesmere Port, Cheshire
Printed and bound in Great Britain by
Billings Bookplan, Worcester

Contents

Preface

Small businesses are not large businesses in microcosm. Their distinctive nature has been recognized by successive governments, financial institutions and by the business community of which they are a part. They form a separate segment of commerce and industry.

Within that segment there is great diversity – of legal status, activity, size and personnel. Despite their diversity, the widespread use of the popular generic terms 'small business' and 'small firm' serves to emphasize that these small enterprises have much in common with one another. We have therefore chosen to use the terms 'business' and 'firm'. Only where it is important to make the distinction have we differentiated between company, partnership or proprietorship.

The men and women responsible for financial management in small businesses are not a homogeneous group. Besides their differences in age and experience, they are known by a variety of titles: financial manager, partner, proprietor, principal, director, to name but a few of them. Some of the titles describe seniority or status or indicate that financial management is only one of several responsibilities. In order to avoid engaging in a lengthy exercise in semantics we have chosen the title 'manager' as that which most aptly identifies and describes the reader.

The style, content and layout of the book are designed to provide for this diversity of business and personnel. Some managers may use the book for self-help independent study. To others it may serve as an off-the-job training text. Other managers will treat it primarily as a reference book.

Students preparing to become the next generation of business managers and technologists with managerial responsibilities will discover that it is a book which relates to real life situations.

Our aim is to provide for diverse needs in a practical way. The book incorporates our complementary experience of small business start-up, management, consultancy and business education.

D. A. Hill and *L. E. Rockley*
Kenilworth 1989

Acknowledgements

We are indebted to Frank Case, an underwriter, John Hallett, a practising professional accountant with a number of small business clients and to Chris Lyon, founder and managing director of Cryslon Sound Systems Ltd. They have read the manuscript, offered comments and made suggestions.

Doug Fox of Heinemann Professional Publishing has given invaluable support when we have needed it.

Part One   Overview

The arena in which financial management operates is constantly moving. It is bounded on the one side by the workings and aspirations of the business itself. The practices of the wider business community – customers, suppliers and financiers together with the rules and regulations associated with the machinery of government – form a second boundary around the arena.

If a business is unsuccessful the boundaries close in. Management has little room to manoeuvre and is subject to increasing pressure.

With success comes a slackening of the boundary ropes at many points. The business is then more at liberty to enjoy the fruits of success as it moves forward to achieve further successes.

1   The scope and context of financial management

This book is not primarily about accounting or book-keeping. It is about financial management in small businesses with up to 200 employees. The size of such businesses may be small but the scope of financial management is wide-ranging. The number of terms and abbreviations bears witness to the scope and diversity encountered in small businesses of which the authors have experience.

The aim of the book is to provide a comprehensive, in-depth, user friendly, practical guide for the manager of a small business. The content of the book, its style and layout take into account the typical small business manager's working day, responsibilities, financial training, experience and needs.

Systematically working through the chapters devoted to the various topics will satisfy the need for an aid to a thorough consideration of all the available options before making a decision. The reference sections at the end of the book complement the preceding chapters and satisfy another need. That is the need for quick access to a jargon-free guide to the abbreviations and terminology circulating in the financial world with which the manager has only occasional contact.

The book is therefore divided into five parts:

1   An overview of small business financial management
2   Financial systems and techniques
3   Specific management tasks
4   Glossary of terms
5   Appendices

Convention, custom and practice have led to considerable overlapping between financial management, accounting and book-keeping. The three functions are closely related but they are not identical. In some businesses one person is responsible for all three functions, but in others book-keeping and accounting are separate from financial management.

The financial manager may not be a trained accountant. Accounting and book-keeping services may be provided by specialist firms and individuals but the responsibility for financial management is an integral part of small business management. It is therefore important to answer the question 'What is financial management?' at the outset.

What is financial management?

There is no universally accepted definition of financial management. Information on possible definitions can be obtained from a number of sources. The contents pages of financial management textbooks, which concentrate on large companies, are one source. Advertisements in newspapers for financial managers, directors and comptrollers are another source and an indication of current thinking on the duties of these people. Dictionaries are the third source of possible definitions.

Among all the different definitions there is a measure of agreement. Financial management is concerned with:

- Specifying and attaining objectives.
- Safeguarding and making optimum use of resources.
- Achieving aims.
- Enabling something to happen according to plans and budgets.

Implied in these phrases taken from the possible sources of definitions are certain concepts. The principal concept is that *financial management is concerned with moving a business forward.* The corollary of this is that it has to create and maintain a financial infrastructure, to organize, to control strategy, make decisions, prevent and overcome obstacles of a financial nature as well as contributing to overcoming non-financial obstacles with financial implications. Accounting for and recording past events is vital for providing statements of the starting and ongoing positions. These change with the passage of time, and need up-to-date management information.

In practical terms this means that financial management has the following duties:

1 The raising and provision of money.
2 The control of the flow of money in the present and future.
3 The stewardship of money already invested in the business.
4 Meeting obligations to suppliers of goods and services, employees, providers of finance and other interested parties (statutory and non-statutory).
5 Protecting the business against financial ills.
6 Achieving financial targets and objectives.
7 Advising colleagues of the financial implications of their plans and decisions.
8 Representing the interests of the business when attending to the financial needs of the business which involve outsiders.

Why is financial management needed?

There are positive as well as negative reasons why a business needs financial management.

It is not a luxury.

Prominent amongst the positive reasons is *the need to consolidate* the different parts of financial management described in the preceding section into a coherent operational strategy. Although all the parts interact, without such consolidation there is a danger of fragmentization with all its associated control problems (such as one department leap-frogging another). This strategy after it has been formulated goes on to form the basis of tactical decisions. These have to be made from time to time to keep the business on course as the business is confronted by changes in circumstances, events and situations, major and minor, expected and unexpected.

Not all those strategic and tactical decisions made by management are financial. There are those which are primarily financial and those with financial implications. It can however be argued that all decisions and actions in a business, if not initially so, are ultimately of a financial nature.

Unfortunately the need for financial management is most strongly supported by reference to what may happen if it is

Exhibit 1.1 *Financial difficulties*

Principal and secondary causes	Consequential effects
1 Short-term liquidity and under capitalization	Sales promotion curtailed by cuts in advertising, exhibiting, publicity and personnel, with secondary effects on order intake after a period of time has elapsed.
1.1 Low stock turnover	Purchasing difficulties as suppliers respond to slow payment record with delayed deliveries and demands for prepayments.
1.2 Insufficient external finance (Note 1.3 below)	Manufacturing difficulties because material shortages delay completion of work and adversely affect the level of service to customers.
1.3 Disproportionately high interest payments	Personnel retention affected by an inability to pay competitive rates, skill shortages follow and there is insufficient money to train new recruits, recruiting new personnel itself being a further drain on liquidity.
1.4 Under utilization of assets, tangible and intangible facilities, space and machines	Payments of interest and repayments of loans are difficult and may lead to litigation.
1.5 Low or unsuitable order book	Market and product development is abandoned or postponed.
1.6 Inaccessible investments	Penalties are applied for late payment of
1.7 Uninsured accidents and business interruptions	
1.8 High wages and salaries but low productivity	
1.9 Defective credit control	
1.10 Theft, fraud and dishonesty	
1.11 Disproportionately high expenditure on development	

2	**Defective management information**	Management is handicapped by lack of information when attempting to deal with other financial difficulties e.g. liquidity problems which necessitate cuts and postponements but which may be effected in the wrong place because guesses have to substitute for informed and considered decisions.
2.1	Shortage of staff	
2.2	Defective procedures	Prices charged may be either too low to provide an adequate return or so high as to deter customers. The secondary effect of this is under-utilization of facilities.
2.3	Inadequate facilities	
2.4	Inappropriate systems	Insufficient costing information is available for the evaluation of alternative methods, materials and processes.
3	**Defective credit control**	Losses due to bad debts.
3.1	Lax procedures	Reduction of liquidity due to customers taking extended payment terms.
3.2	Misplaced confidence in customers	Adverse effects on cash flow.
4	**Theft, fraud and dishonesty**	Erosion of profit margins.
4.1	Inadequate internal auditing	Reduction of liquidity due to reduced cash balances.
4.2	Defective recruitment and selection	In extreme cases – cessation of trading.
4.3	Inadequate insurance cover	

lacking or absent altogether. Financial management is *needed to prevent a business succumbing* to those factors which have been on many occasions identified as the reasons why businesses have ceased to trade.

Exhibit 1.1 shows that the majority of the reasons for business failure and difficulties are of a financial nature. Although causes and effects are listed separately, if the situation is left uncorrected it gathers momentum and reaches the point where cause and effect are indistinguishable from one another in a vortex of financial problems. Although financial management cannot avoid all problems, it can fulfil a need by avoiding many and controlling the majority of those remaining even if they are unavoidable. The section on contingency planning in Chapter 10 is relevant to the controlling of unavoidable problems.

Exhibit 1.2 is the counterpart of Exhibit 1.1. It lists some causes and consequences which have financial implications. If financial management is not needed to deal with these causes and consequences it is needed to alert the managers responsible for dealing with them to their financial implications for the business as a whole.

A strategy for financial management

Financial management is therefore needed to make a major contribution to the management of the whole business. It must of necessity be seen to be part of the whole business and not an outlier.

Firstly, financial management needs to have a *status* which is in accordance with its importance. As the results of the activities of, for example, marketing and manufacturing managers are more easily and quickly measured than those of their financial counterpart, it is unfortunately not unusual for them and their managers to be given an elevated status in a business. The financial manager is disadvantaged if this occurs.

Secondly, to prevent the occurrence of this disadvantage the second part of the strategy for financial management is needed. Financial management needs *integration* with the activities of other departments, not isolation from them. If it is isolated there is a danger of inter-departmental confrontation which has to be resolved by management intervention.

Thirdly, financial management needs *resources* in the form of personnel, equipment and facilities. The money spent on these resources has to be measured against their actual benefits. Whilst the emphasis is on the positive benefits of financial management, the protective ones cannot be ignored. Without such protection the foundations of the business may be undermined.

Fourthly, financial management needs *application* to the key issues affecting the pulse of the business. A typical key issue in a small business, which involves the majority if not all the duties of financial management and has implications for other departments, is bank borrowing. There are two aspects to bank borrowing. On the one hand it is a facility for enabling a business to help itself by grasping opportunities earlier than would be the case if the business had to rely on its own resources. On the other hand it can be a liability with ramifications affecting inventory management, sales promotion, recruitment and training of personnel, the payment of wages, capital expenditure and purchases. If bank borrowing is approaching an agreed limit, a ceiling has to be applied to all these activities. There are other examples of key issues for the application of financial management 'e.g. overseeing an expansion programme, arranging to move a business or acquire other businesses are key issues which cross departmental boundaries.

Financial objectives and their implications

Besides its duties, benefits and relationships, there are three other elements which help define the context of financial management. The first of these elements are the financial objectives within which it has to operate. These objectives differ greatly between businesses. The difference affects many aspects of financial management not least its style, time-scales, and policies. The following is a representative list of objectives:

1 A stable steady income with the emphasis on stability rather than growth.

Exhibit 1.2 *Difficulties with financial implications*

Principal and secondary causes	*Consequential effects*
1 Inefficient production	
1.1 Low or unsuitable order book	Unit costs are unacceptably high.
1.2 Defective inventory management	Sales are depressed by high prices having to compensate for the production inefficiencies.
1.3 Inadequate production planning and control	Inability to respond quickly to customers' acceptable lead times diverts sales to competitors.
1.4 Inappropriate methods	Under utilization of machinery, and labour.
1.5 Inappropriate machinery	Poor quality.
1.6 Inefficient workplace layout	Unjustified overtime at premium rates to make up for the shortfalls.
1.7 Unsuitable labour	Profit margins are depressed if market prices are charged but production and manufacturing costs exceed those of competitors.
1.8 Unreliable machinery	

2	Uneven customer base	
2.1	Ineffective sales direction and promotion	Sales are depressed.
2.2	Failure to respond to changes in the market place	Difficulty in attracting new customers and promotion of growth.
2.3	Failure to introduce new products and update existing ones	
2.4	Insufficient market research	
3	Uneven product base	The future prospects for the business are uncertain due to the possible impact of
3.1	Insufficient research and development	technological changes, sales, and customer preferences.
3.2	Inadequate manufacturing facilities to produce a family of related products	Production facilities cannot be diverted to other products to reduce the impact of the above if there are no alternatives available.
3.3	Insufficient labour with the requisite skills of producing what the market is demanding	Labour and assets cannot be used effectively nor overheads recovered.

2 High income whether the business is starting, newly acquired or at some other stage of development.
3 Steady growth without recourse to external finance so that management enjoys considerable independence.
4 Profitable exit from the business (e.g. via the third market or unlisted securities market or by a privately arranged sale) so that capital gains may be made.
5 Putting the interest of the controlling family first.
6 Occasionally the principal of a business has political ambitions so the objective of the business is to make a contribution to a publicly acceptable high profile.
7 A small minority see the objective of the business as providing a hobby for the principal.

Businesses with clearly defined short term ambitious objectives tend to have an aggressive management style. Time scales are short, assessments of performance penetrating, while the policy towards risks may be bold and targets resolutely pursued.

Those with more modest objectives have a more relaxed style, possibly paternalistic, and one which is less overtly resolute in the pursuit of its objectives. Caution replaces boldness so plans are slowly formulated and very thoroughly investigated and appraised. Liquidity is of paramount importance as is the provision for unforeseen eventualities.

External constraints

Whatever its objectives and management style, no small business is free from constraints. There are those constraints which are external to it and there are internal ones within the business. On page 5 reference was made to meeting obligations to several interested parties. These apply to all businesses whether they be sole proprietorships, partnerships, limited companies, co-operatives or friendly societies.

Statutory obligations are the principal constraint on financial management. All businesses must answer to the Inland Revenue and usually to Customs and Excise as the majority are registered for VAT. Limited companies in return for the privilege of limited liability, which is often curtailed in practice by financial institutions, have to file annual accounts with the Registrar of Companies under threat of penalties for default specified by the Companies Acts. Directors of companies are subject to the Company Director's Disqualification Act 1986 and the Insolvency Act 1986. Compliance with these constraints is incumbent upon financial management.

There is also a hidden external constraint. Credit agencies, corporate raiders and predators may without the knowledge of a limited company consult the filed accounts. There are small businesses who decide against incorporation in order to safeguard themselves from the clandestine attentions of those who peruse the accounts of limited companies.

Internal constraints

Internal constraints are much more diverse and imprecise than the external ones. Their absence or presence shows whether there is a strategy for financial management. If there is an inadequate strategy, financial management will be constrained by inadequate resources, lack of direction and a lowly status. It will only become important if there is a financial crisis.

The lack of opportunity for advancement and the small scope for exercising financial management skills cause many financially qualified personnel to prefer employment in larger companies and professional firms. Unfortunately the resources of the majority of small businesses are too small for them to use outside consultants to compensate for this financial management deficiency. Managers trained in other disciplines have therefore to take financial management on board and maybe combine it with other duties.

This book is intended to assist people who are in such situations. It aims to be a source of guidance and reference for those who are determined to be successful despite all the constraints, problems and difficulties often encountered in managing a small business.

The hallmark of success

Financial management is successful when all the constraints

are under control, the procedures working, employees, customers, suppliers and providers of finance, whatever their identity, confident that the business is achieving its current financial objectives and is on course for the realization of future ones. The cash position of the business is a good indication of its health.

Part Two   Financial Systems and Techniques

The financial systems and techniques constitute the machinery of financial management – an understanding of which is necessary for success.

The help of computers may be enlisted for those tasks which are routine *provided the safeguards recommended are in operation.*

2   The analysis of profit

The manager of the average small business is not required to be trained in the processes of accountancy – nor is it essential that she or he should be. They may employ the services of a firm of accountants to

1   Produce books of accounts.
2   Present statements:
    (a)   of the business's possessions and liabilities, and
    (b)   of the periodic profit or loss state of its trading operations, and
    (c)   to prepare taxation computations for the Inland Revenue.

It is the understanding of items (a) and (b) above, and how to utilize the data given therein, in the effective management of the business, which must be the prime objective of the small business manager and therefore of our early studies.

The Glossary contains brief definitions of the terms and ratios discussed below. These are:

Terms

Assets
Asset backing
Capital employed
Current assets
Current liabilities
Depreciation

Intangible assets
Net worth
Tangible asset
Working capital
Work in progress

Ratios

Acid test   Quick ratio
Current ratio   Turnover of capital employed

The other key ratios are discussed below.
Relevant computer programs are in Part Five, Appendix 1.

The balance sheet

A balance sheet, or statement of affairs as it may well be described, shows the value of a firm's possessions and of its liabilities at some past date. It is essentially a backward looking document which shows the business's wealth at that past date only. Eventually we must consider how we may construct a prospective *future balance sheet* which would attempt to predict the results deriving from the actions of present business policies.

Exhibit 2.1 *The Small Trading Co.*

Balance Sheet as at 31st March 19...

| Items on this side show where the firm's capital, its borrowings and trade credits came from. | Items on this side show how the total amount of funds and credit was used: it details the assets of the business at the above date. |

Exhibit 2.1 is merely a simple explanation of the contents of a conventional two-sided 'statement of affairs'. But the reader must study Exhibit 2.2 to see how practical data of any firm's possessions – long life assets plus stocks and debtors – together with the related financing services are recorded.

'Capital' is a term which is usually qualified, e.g. share capital or working capital (see page 181) because it is somewhat vague. It usually represents the tangible resources of a business.

Exhibit 2.2 has given life to the 'statement of affairs' by

Exhibit 2.2 *The Small Trading Co.*
Balance sheet as at 31st March 19...

		£				£
1	Manager's initial investment	30,000	8	Land and buildings		30,000
2	Profits retained in business	5,000	9	Plant and machinery		10,000
3	Money borrowed	20,000	10	Vehicles		2,000
4	Capital invested for the long term	55,000	11	Business assets of expected long lives		42,000
5	Creditors (for trade supplies)	£ 8,000	12	Stocks (materials, work in progress, finished goods)	£ 13,000	
6	Bank overdraft	7,000	13	Debtors	15,000	
7	Short-term financing	15,000				28,000
		£70,000				£70,000

Note: Item 12. Only manufacturers are likely to have work in progress. The same comment applies to Exhibit 2.6.

incorporating specimen figures. At this stage the reader should examine his or her own business position when it is expressed in similar terms and groupings. Clearly the long-term invested capital must earn an acceptable rate of return.

For example, £55,000 could earn, if it was invested★ in:

1	A Building Society at 7.5%	£4,125
2	National Savings Certificates at 5.5% tax free	£3,025
3	Government Income Bonds at 9% (pre-tax)	£4,950
4	Gilt Edged Stock at, say, 10% (pre-tax)	£5,500

The conclusion to be drawn, from these readily available samples, would be that if the business was making a pre-tax profit less than these amounts, the manager is working for nothing.

The profit and loss account

So the term 'profit' has crept into the evaluation of our business' performance and therefore we must immediately direct our reading to an easy familiarity with the content and layout of a conventional profit and loss account.

Exhibit 2.3 *Profit and loss account for the year ended ......*

Expenditure	*Income*
Cost of goods and service *consumed* – during the period shown above – in producing the goods and services which generated the income.	Income earning output (e.g. sales) *achieved* during that same period.

It will not be difficult to see that when income exceeds expenditure, profit results. Conversely, a loss will arise when the figures show that expenditure exceeds income. But a note of caution is essential here. The profit and loss accounts does

★ At the time of reading this section, the business executive should ascertain the then current investment rates available.

not record cash receipts and payments: it is a record of income and expenditure as defined in the above exhibit. A study of cash flow and its measurement will be dealt with later.

But prior to our studies of cash flow we must give life to Exhibit 2.3 by presenting a suggested profit and loss account, containing some appropriate financial data, for The Small Trading Co. Here the reader should understand that the profit and loss account in Exhibit 2.4 shows the operating efficiency of the business in the period leading up to the date of the balance sheet given in Exhibit 2.2.

Exhibit 2.4 *The Small Trading Co.*
Profit and loss account for the year ended March ......

Expenditure	£	Income	£
Wages	10,000	Sales	40,000
Supplies	20,000		
Miscellaneous	500		
Depreciation	2,500		
Interest	2,500		
	35,500		
Profit before tax C/D	4,500		
	£40,000		£40,000
Taxation (say 25%)	1,125	Profit before tax B/D	4,500
Profit after tax	3,375		
	£4,500		£4,500

Return on capital employed (ROCE)

The balance sheet and its related profit and loss account (given in Exhibits 2.2 and 2.4) do not contain a great amount of detail. They are adequate enough, however, to enable the demonstrations of certain basic ratio analyses which can be defined and used, with ease, in the ongoing management of any business.

The Small Trading Co., with its pre-tax profit of £4,500, may be said to be barely justifying its business continuance.

Therefore we must set out the essential processes which will enable us to:

1   Appraise the past performance of the business.
2   Identify those areas of activity which demand the attention of management in order to improve its future profitability.

Capital employed

The term 'capital employed' is widely used in the assessment of trading performance. It is defined as:

1   Capital invested for the long term (i.e. £55,000 in Exhibit 2.2), *or*
2   Long life assets plus★ working capital (i.e. £42,000 plus £28,000 − £15,000).

Matched against the total of capital employed we shall set the profit before tax and interest which is demonstrated in the related profit and loss account. Thus the state of operating efficiency of The Small Trading Co. is represented by:

$$\frac{\text{profit before tax and interest} \times 100}{\text{capital employed}} = \frac{7,000 \times 100}{55,000} = 12.72\%$$

and the 12.72% is termed *the return on capital employed*.

Here the reader should understand why the profit figure used in the above calculation is the amount derived from before tax *and* before interest. This stand is taken because:

1   Interest costs are regarded as a financing cost, *not* as an operation cost, *and*
2   When comparing the performance of a smaller business with those of larger firms or limited companies, we find that the profit ratio used by such larger firms will always be before interest.

At the same time it is interesting to note that if we used a profit before tax figure of only £,4500), then the return on capital

★ Working capital is defined as those assets of shorter lives (stocks plus debtors plus cash) less those liabilities which demand reasonably early settlement (creditors plus bank overdraft).

would be a mere 8.18%! While the impact of borrowings will be dealt with in a separate analysis, the manager of the small business must be made aware of the potentially serious impact of excessive interest charges upon ultimate gain. See Exhibit 9.2 below for an illustration.

A study of ROCE shows that the overall business return is affected by the:

1 Return of sales, *and*
2 Sales per £ of capital employed (capital turnover).

This most important relationship between profit, capital employed and sales is demonstrated in this equation:

Exhibit 2.5 *The Small Trading Co.*
Sources of profit growth

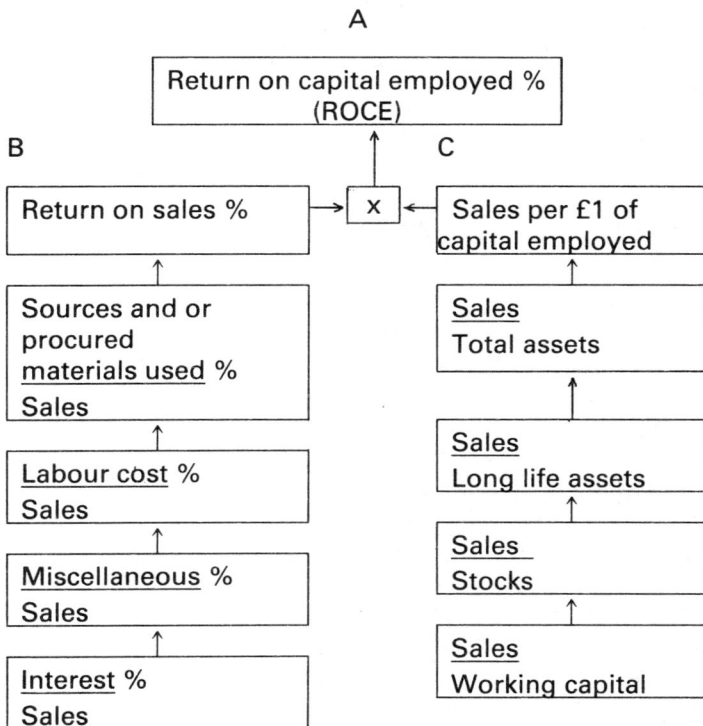

A

Return on capital employed % (ROCE)

B   C

| Return on sales % | → | X | ← | Sales per £1 of capital employed |

| Sources and or procured materials used % Sales | | Sales Total assets |

| Labour cost % Sales | | Sales Long life assets |

| Miscellaneous % Sales | | Sales Stocks |

| Interest % Sales | | Sales Working capital |

$$\frac{\text{profit} \times 100}{\text{capital employed}} = \frac{\text{profit} \times 100}{\text{sales}} \times \frac{\text{sales}}{\text{capital employed}}$$

which is described as:

$$\frac{\text{percentage return}}{\text{on capital employed}} = \frac{\text{percentage return}}{\text{on sales}} \times \frac{\text{sales per £1 of}}{\text{capital employed}}$$

The next stage in our search for factors affecting a business's profitability involves extending this ROCE equation. Thus, Exhibit 2.5 shows how we can find out the underlying reasons for our current profit performance, even though we have but the limited data recorded in Exhibits 2.2 and 2.4.

There are few businesses to which the majority of the above ratios do not refer. The difference is in the emphasis which they attract either for the business as a whole or for one department of it. The exhibit confirms that sales are at the heart of financial management.

So far as the rate of profit on sales goes, we can follow the process of searching for greater profitability if we now use the figures given in our simple profit and loss account in Exhibit 2.4.

$$\frac{\text{materials used or procured} \times 100}{\text{sales}} = \frac{20,000 \times 100}{40,000} = \quad 50\%$$

$$\frac{\text{labour cost} \times 100}{\text{sales}} = \frac{10,000 \times 100}{40,000} = \quad 25\%$$

$$\frac{\text{miscellaneous costs} \times 100}{\text{sales}} = \frac{500 \times 100}{40,000} = 1.25\%$$

$$\frac{\text{interest costs} \times 100}{\text{sales}} = \frac{2,500 \times 100}{40,000} = 6.25\%$$

Clearly the business manager must be able to obtain a more detailed cost (expenditure) structure in order to extend any enquiries. The importance of this analysis, however, is that it should be done regularly, e.g. monthly or quarterly. By these means a continuing watch can be kept for any changing incidence of the various cost impacts upon profit. Furthermore, it surely need not be over-emphasized that any emerging loss tendencies (i.e., from growing cost percentage factors) should be dealt with promptly.

Measuring the effective use of assets (see Exhibits 1.1–1.4)

The effective use of assets is particularly important where there is substantial investment in premises and equipment, e.g. hotels, the leisure industry, process plant, sophisticated machine tools or warehouses.

Our search for a higher return on capital employed does not end with an analysis of the profit on sales. Our balance sheet shows that we have invested in assets which the business appears to need in creating its saleable goods, products and services. The importance of this factor is shown by the capital turnover element of ROCE. It shows the extent to which the creation of sales has demanded the availability of assets for the firm's output to be completed and financed. So we return to Exhibit 2.5, group C, and insert the related sales/asset valuations, which have been given, for each asset group: here the sales value created, *per* £, of each asset group is clearly stated.

$$\frac{\text{sales}}{\text{total assets}} = \frac{£40,000}{70,000} = \begin{array}{l}£0.57 \text{ of sales} \\ \text{per } £1 \text{ of assets}\end{array}$$

$$\frac{\text{sales}}{\text{long life assets}} = \frac{£40,000}{42,000} = \begin{array}{l}£0.95 \text{ of sales} \\ \text{per } £1 \text{ of long} \\ \text{life assets}\end{array}$$

$$\frac{\text{sales}}{\text{stocks}} = \frac{£40,000}{13,000} = \begin{array}{l}£3.08 \text{ of sales per} \\ £1 \text{ of stocks}\end{array}$$

$$\frac{\text{sales}}{\text{debtors}} = \frac{£40,000}{15,000} = \begin{array}{l}£2.67 \text{ of sales per} \\ £1 \text{ of debtors}\end{array}$$

$$\frac{\text{sales}}{\text{working capital}} = \frac{£40,000}{13,000} = \begin{array}{l}£3.08 \text{ of sales per} \\ £1 \text{ of working capital}\end{array}$$

Even with these sparse figures it is evident that the land and buildings, plant, equipment and vehicles do not generate that value of output which could secure a sales income sufficient to finance their replacement, modernization or improvement. The vastly changing competitive circumstances of modern business demand that the business manager must examine the operational activity of any long life assets.* Are they each

* Generally termed the 'fixed assets' of the business.

being used fully or at all? If it is found that certain items of plant, equipment or parts of premises and machinery remain idle or unused for long periods of the year, the question to be asked is 'do we need them?' It may be that their rarely used function can be more cheaply obtained from an outside contractor.

Further, the cash received from the sales of surplus, or unrequired, machinery or equipment may produce the funds to (a) pay off some loans and thus reduce interest charges or (b) to pay off creditors and thus enhance the business's credit rating with its suppliers and, essentially, with its bankers! Alternatively steps may be taken to improve the utilization of such assets to justify their retention.

Working capital management

Though the business manager may ever be concerned with improving profitability, she or he must also have the objective of *staying* in business, i.e. solvency. But this aim does *not* direct action from the creation of profit, for we have seen how we can investigate the sales generating power of the fixed assets. Thus we must also consider how effectively our working capital is being used.

The sales generated per £1 of working capital has been noted above but this overall turnover rate can hide the adverse effects of one of the various constituents of working capital.

Turnover of working capital

This ratio has been presented earlier as 'sales per £ of working capital', thus evidencing the value of sales which are under-pinned by £1 worth of working capital. The turnover rate thus given – £3.08 – shows that working capital is 32.47% of sales (100 ÷ 3.08) and the rate must be regarded as somewhat high for a manufacturing company: it would be considered excessive for a service company.

Turnover of stocks

This is particularly important for manufacturers and distributors. Some businesses in the service sector have negligible stocks. (See Exhibits 1.1–1.4.)

Here an analysis of the term 'stocks' into their separate constituents of:

- Raw material
- Work in progress
- Finished goods

will enable us to show whether the rate of turnover of each item of stock is acceptable or whether too great a value of one type of stock is being held, thus adversely affecting the firm's profitability and solvency aims.

The rate of turnover of each of the separate items will tell us how long the various items of stock remained on the premises, i.e. were not converted into goods sold – the source of the business's income. Here it is emphasized that we shall use the value of the *average* stock held in order to arrive at this most important element in the drive for business profitability. In our subsequent calculations the values of the separate types of stock will be taken to be:

	January 1st £	December 31st £
Raw materials	6,000	8,000
Work in progress	3,000	4,000
Finished goods	3,000	1,000
	12,000	13,000*

The figures assumed for January 1st have been used because our balance sheet in Exhibit 2.2 sets out the position at the year end, December 31st. In a practical situation the business manager should have comparable information for each which will enable a closer watch on any adverse stockholding trends.

Before proceeding to our turnover rate calculations, we must first insert the above stockholding values for January 1st and December 31st into an extended version of our simple profit and loss account given in exhibit 2.4. The result, now

* See Exhibit 2.2.

Exhibit 2.6 *The Small Trading Co.*
Trading and profit and loss account for the year ended 31st December 19...

	£	£	£
Materials consumed			
Opening stock	6,000		
Purchases	22,000		
	28,000		
Less closing stock	8,000	20,000	
Wages		10,000	
Prime cost		30,000	

	£		
Overheads:			
Miscellaneous	250		
Depreciation	500	750	
		30,750	

Add work in progress 1st January		3,000	
		33,750	
Less work in progress 31st December		4,000	
Product cost		29,750	
Add finished goods 1st January		3,000	
		32,750	
Less finished goods 31st December		1,000	
Cost of sales		31,750	Sales 40,000
Gross profit carried down		8,250	
		40,000	40,000
			Gross profit brought down 8,250
Administration overheads	250		
Depreciation	2,000		
Interest	2,500	4,750	
Profit before tax		3,500	
		£8,250	£8,250

entitled a trading and profit and loss account, is given in Exhibit 2.6 opposite.

Using Exhibit 2.6, the reader is directed to a study of the terms:

Prime cost   Services and materials used (or procured) + labour cost.

Product cost   Prime cost + overhead + January 1st work in progress − December 31st work in progress.

Cost of Sales   Product cost + January 1st finished goods − December 31st finished goods.

So we can now proceed to a practical assessment of the turnover rates for each of the main classes of stockholding. Here the comparable data to be used in our calculations are:

    Raw materials   with materials consumed.
    Work in progress   with cost of goods manufactured.
    Finished goods   with cost of goods sold.

Raw materials turnover

$$\frac{\text{materials consumed}}{\text{average raw material stocks}} = \frac{20,000}{(6,000 + 8,000) \div 2}$$

$$= \frac{20,000}{7,000} = \begin{array}{l} 2.86 \text{ times in the} \\ \text{operating period} \end{array}$$

This means that a stock unit or component would tend to remain in the stores for* *128 days on average!* This is a high statement of stockholding days and must have a costly impact on the firm's operations. Taking advantage of quantity discounts may be unwise. Buying smaller quantities from wholesalers may be preferable.

---

   * The stockholding days are arrived at by dividing the number of days in the period by the period's turnover rate (365 ÷ 2.86). If the period under examination had been one quarter, the calculations would have been 91 ÷ 2.86.

Work in progress turnover

$$\frac{\text{total manufacturing costs of the output}}{\text{average work in progress stocks}} = \frac{29,750}{(3,000+4,000)\div 2}$$

$$= \frac{29.750}{3,500} = \begin{array}{l} 8.5 \text{ times in the} \\ \text{operating period} \end{array}$$

Here we can express the turnover rate as the number of days *on average* that a piece of work in progress remains in work in progress, here, 43 days. This would need investigation by the manager for, such a turnover rate is, again, high. The introduction of AMT (advanced manufacturing technology) is frequently justified on the grounds of the reduction in work in progress which it is capable of achieving even for small businesses.

Finished goods turnover

$$\frac{\text{Cost of goods sold}}{\text{average finished goods stocks}} = \frac{31,750}{(3,000+1,000)\div 2}$$

$$= \frac{31.750}{2,000} = \begin{array}{l} 15.9 \text{ times in the} \\ \text{operating period} \end{array}$$

This represents a finished goods turnover rate as 23 days approximately.
. In circumstances such as these action is needed for better stock control. It will mean careful examination of strategies, procedures for purchasing further raw materials, progressing of goods from suppliers or being manufactured and the selling of the finished goods. It may be considered that the management of finished goods stock is improving, as the value of finished goods in hand has fallen from £3,000 to £1,000. The value of the other categories of stock has increased during the year, and must involve undesirable costs of holding stores, and delays in completing orders due to shortages of isolated items.

Cash flow problems

We continue the examination of working capital impacts upon business profitability by studying the turnover rates of the essentially cash based elements of working capital. Here we shall identify the extent of the delays in receipts of *cash* for goods sold and delivered to customers, and the delays in payment by the firm for materials and components it has itself received.

Firstly, it must be emphasized that long delays in the settlement of accounts by customers must cost money. These extra costs or lost profits will arise from

1   An increase in the bank overdraft of the business.
2   The need to borrow money elsewhere, perhaps on a long-term basis.
3   An inability to finance a full manufacturing capacity or service facility.
4   Less money available for placing on deposit or investing.

Turnover of debtors

In this ratio we divide the total *credit* sales by the book value of the debtors outstanding at the end of the operating period.

$$\frac{\text{sales}}{\text{debtors}} = \frac{40{,}000 \text{ (Exhibit 2.4)}}{15{,}000 \text{ (Exhibit 2.2)}} = \begin{array}{l} 2.67 \text{ times in the} \\ \text{operating period} \end{array}$$

Using the method shown in the stock turnover calculations, we can convert the rating into the average day's credit being allowed to customers. This is shown by 365 ÷ 2.67 = 137 days! Clearly this is far too high, coming to a credit allowed period of over four months *on average*.

Whether this situation exists throughout the year can be verified by a regular monthly aged debtor analysis (see Glossary) or 'audit' of the firm's outstanding debtors. They should be listed in groups of debtors remaining unpaid for, say, two, three and four months. Thus we may identify the more troublesome customers, especially if the firm's quoted credit period offered to customers is only thirty days.

Turnover of creditors

On the other hand, the business manager may act to delay payment of creditors in order to ease cash flow problems. We do not recommend such a policy here. The loss of the firm's credit rating may result in reluctant suppliers:

1   Delaying the provision of essential services and materials.
2   Increasing ('loading') their supply prices.
3   Cancelling credit terms or lowering credit limits.

These circumstances must lead to reduced profitability for the small business.

The turnover of creditors is calculated by dividing the period's total raw material (and component) purchases by the related trade creditors outstanding at the end of the operating period.

$$\frac{\text{purchases}}{\text{debtors}} = \frac{22,200 \text{ (Exhibit 2.6)}}{8,000 \text{ (Exhibit 2.2)}} = \begin{array}{l} 2.75 \text{ times in the} \\ \text{operating period} \end{array}$$

Again we can find that the average day's credit allowed by, or taken from, suppliers is $365 \div 2.75 = 132.7$ days.

Conclusions

A comparison of the debtor and creditor turnover rates gives the impression that the former is affecting the latter! On the other hand, the circumstances outlined above – the turnover of debtors and creditors – may arise from a continuous, or rapid, expansion of business without

1   Securing, beforehand, a sufficient operating capital to sustain the extra business. (See Exhibits 1.1–1.2.)
2   Paying sufficient attention to the firm's credit rating – which is just as important as an effective manufacturing cost control.

Clearly we now need to direct our studies to cost control and effective budgeting, at least for the current, and the next, operating periods.

Financial or business planning is not the same as budgeting.

The former concentrates on the whole business whereas budgeting concentrates on the constituent parts (see Chapter 10) of it.

3   Cost accounting I

Chapter 2 has been concerned with analysing the overall financial state of the business. The balance sheet presents an asset/liability state at the year end while the profit and loss account reports the total gain or loss during that year. These statements – particularly the profit and loss account – are referred to as the 'financial accounts'. Now financial accounts do not examine the various operations of the business *in detail*: they are concerned with the *whole business* though in some larger firms financial accounts may be designed to identify the worth of various divisions or sections of the entire business.

Therefore in order to identify the sources of a business's profit (or loss), its strengths and weaknesses and to improve its performance, we must set out to obtain more detailed information about the cost of:

1   Operating individual departments or services, on and off site.
2   Providing products and services to customers.
3   Obtaining goods and services from suppliers.

Cost accounts can be structured to produce a more detailed and continuous reporting of the business's affairs, particularly of its profit earning capabilities or to form the basis of quotations to customers.

Cost accounting is a time-consuming activity. Consequently small business managers are tempted to forego it and let the market fix the selling price. (See Exhibits 1.1–1.2.)

Such a practice can be dangerous because it means that there are no internal yardsticks and mechanisms with which to control costs in the short term at the required level of detail for investigations. The manager could be living in a 'fool's paradise' if costs imperceptibly increased and overtook selling prices.

When a costing system is working well, reference to the prevailing market prices, where this is possible, provides a useful source of comparative information. It either confirms or challenges the costings generated by a business. Selling prices may be too low or too high.

There is a considerable number of specialist terms associated with costing. The following are briefly defined in the Glossary:

Absorption costing	Incremental costs
Controllable cost	Indirect labour cost
Contribution	Job costing
Costing	Labour efficiency variances
Cost of sales	Marginal costing
Depreciation	Opportunity cost
Direct costing	Overhead cost
Direct labour costs	Period cost
Direct material	Process costing
Factory cost	Quantity variance
Factory overhead	Semi variable cost
Fixed charges	Standard costing
Fixed costs	Sunk cost
Historical costing	Time cost

Several of the above terms have been excluded from the body of the chapter because they relate only to manufacturing. Those applicable to the majority of small businesses are discussed in more detail below.

The nature of costs

Analysing the costs of business operations, the effects of trade expansions and declines and the preparation of budgets for future activities, can be accomplished only when the nature of each of the cost groups is thoroughly understood.

Fixed costs

These are the costs which are incurred on behalf of the whole business. They do not relate to any single particular product or service. The total value of fixed costs is not affected by variations in the volume of the business's output *unless* such a variation necessitates an increase in its total capacity, e.g. additional premises. In these instances the so called fixed costs will grow also until they settle at a new, higher, level.

Fixed costs cover such items as:

- Supervisory wages and salaries.
- Depreciation of premises and equipment.
- Routine maintenance of equipment.
- Light, heat, power, rent, rates and insurances.
- Sales promotion (excluding campaigns and one-off advertising).

Variable costs

Here we refer to those costs (materials, labour and essential related expenses) which are clearly incurred *solely* because goods are produced or services offered. Variable costs do not arise from the overall structure of the business or from *any other* of its operations. Thus the reader will understand that total variable costs will vary in direct proportion to variations in activity. In theory a doubling of activity will result in doubling of, e.g. materials consumption, labour hours or facilities. In practice there may be lower material costs owing to larger quantities but higher labour costs because it may be necessary to employ contract or agency labour at premium rates or pay premium rates to the employees of the business for overtime working.

Semi-variable costs

This type of cost is partly fixed and partly variable. An example of a semi-variable cost can be taken from the telephone bill which is composed of a fixed rental or standing charge, and an additional charge for each call made.

Other examples of this category of cost will be evident to the business manager. Nevertheless the manager is advised to direct the main management thrust to the variable and fixed categories of cost which have been outlined above. It may be argued that the semi-variable items should be grouped in the fixed cost category – as this is easier for the smaller business.

Product cost

It goes without saying that all the costs of a business – fixed, variable and semi-variable – must be recovered from sales of the goods produced. In this way only can continuing business profitability be achieved.

There may be *occasional* exceptions to this basic rule and they may refer to a policy of setting:

1 Prices below total cost, in order to give an initial impetus to launching a new product or service.
2 Lower prices (and margins) in order to counteract the activities of a major competitor where price is more important than delivery and quality.

The manager must accept that goods manufactured in house should not be sold at prices below their *variable cost* of production whatever the pressures from the sales department because these costs are the inescapable extra expenses which arise from the production itself. To sell below variable costs merely guarantees a manufacturing loss, and a reduction in any overall profit which the firm is currently making.

The reader is now directed to a study of Exhibit 3.1 where the analysis and separation of the several costs of business activity – in a manufacturing or service industry is explained.

Apportioning overhead costs

In all price setting decisions which the manager faces, he or she needs to secure sound present – and future – data of the total overhead costs of the whole business unit. Then he or she will be faced with the problem of deciding upon the most realistic method of allocating such total overheads among each of the products which the firm makes.

Sharing or apportioning overhead costs among the various products can be accomplished in various ways. Three methods of overhead costs allocation are:

Exhibit 3.1 *Allocations of costs*

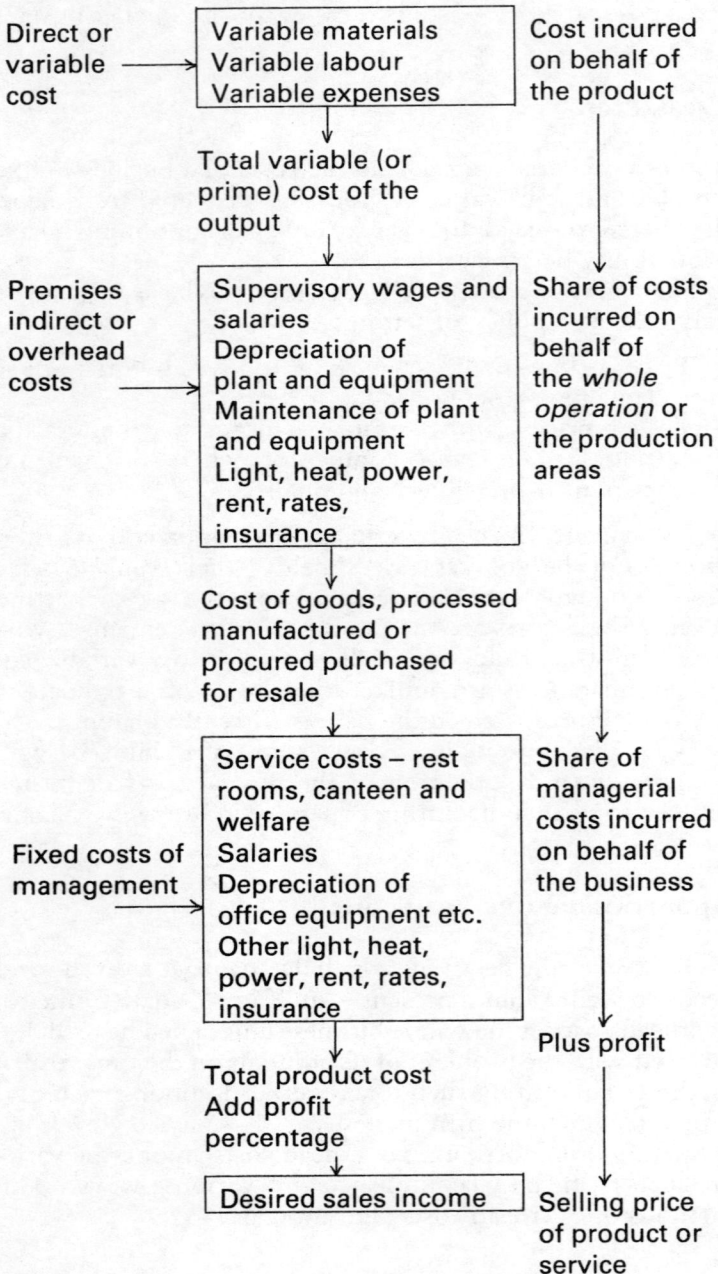

Direct or variable cost →	Variable materials Variable labour Variable expenses	Cost incurred on behalf of the product

↓

Total variable (or prime) cost of the output

↓

Premises indirect or overhead costs →	Supervisory wages and salaries Depreciation of plant and equipment Maintenance of plant and equipment Light, heat, power, rent, rates, insurance	Share of costs incurred on behalf of the *whole operation* or the production areas

↓

Cost of goods, processed manufactured or procured purchased for resale

↓

Fixed costs of management →	Service costs – rest rooms, canteen and welfare Salaries Depreciation of office equipment etc. Other light, heat, power, rent, rates, insurance	Share of managerial costs incurred on behalf of the business

↓

Total product cost
Add profit percentage

Plus profit

↓

| Desired sales income |

Selling price of product or service

1 Direct labour hours.
2 Machine hour rate.
3 Direct labour cost.

There are other systems in use, but a study of the three suggested methods will give the manager a knowledge of the principles to be established in an easy, effective, overhead cost allocation. Time is arguably the easiest basis of apportionment to use in practice. It covers everything from a skilled artisan to a mainframe computer to a customer at a restaurant table.

Direct labour hours

The term 'direct' is defined in the Glossary. Its meaning is very wide.

An examination of the fixed overhead costs given in Exhibit 2.6 together with the manager's knowledge of the cost constituents of the business, will show that many overheads aggregate with the passing of time. So if we can determine the time taken to make or hold a product or give a service and if we then *share out our overheads to products or services accordingly* we shall have a reasonable method of recovering these fixed costs in our pricing policy. Changes in the number of direct hours worked affect overhead recovery.

Direct labour hours involved should be available from

- Employees' time cards, and/or
- Times recorded by employees on the appropriate job sheets, or work schedules.

Direct labour hours is an easy and effective way of determining a basic principle for sharing out the total overhead costs in a business. It is not restricted to manufacturing.

A word of warning is relevant here, however. It may be that in manufacturing business some products are subjected to differing machining operations. Therefore where some automation is involved, e.g. machine utilization/usage times will be a more important factor than labour in any allocation of overhead costs. So our next method of sharing factory overhead costs, for product pricing, should always be borne in mind.

Machine hour rate

Again we propose a time-based criterion in determining the number of hours of *machine time*, which a product demands at a given level of efficiency.

Machine efficiency and machine utilization are not synonymous. A machine may be in use all the time but performing inefficiently, i.e. below expectations.

This does not involve the *cost* of running the machine(s) used in the manufacturing process. It is a method of establishing the period during which the product being manufactured demands the availability of the firm's services of machinery, equipment and their maintenance. Furthermore, a machine hour rate system of overhead cost allocation will be more realistic where employees operate more than one machine. Here overhead cost allocation to products will be the better accomplished where machining time (rather than labour time) is taken as the relevant sharing out criterion.

Direct labour cost

The direct labour *cost* is not the most effective method of allocating overhead costs among the various factory products, *unless* the wages of the whole labour force engaged in manufacture are based upon similar rates. Clearly it is essential for us to share out our time-based overhead costs in a way which results in an equitable division of the total factory overheads among the various items being produced.

The effect of size and diversity

Thus far, the sharing of identified overhead costs, amongst the units of output, has been relatively straightforward. We have directed our analysis to those costs found in smaller businesses, most likely concerned with a single product or service. At most our subject businesses may be concerned with two or three very similar items. Now it is essential that our thinking should be directed to the principal reasons for our concern with overhead cost allocation. The reasons are to:

1 Enable better cost control.
2 Identify the *whole* cost of each item of the output.
3 Avoid selling at a loss in the future.

As our smaller business grows in size it may become involved with a range of products. As a result of some diversification it will employ a variety of equipment for different processes, for the stages contributing to the emergence of the ultimate product. The additional equipment types suggested here may include such tasks as:

- Machining
- Drilling
- Welding
- Polishing
- Pressing
- Soldering

These are a few of the more familiar equipment-based operations which serve to illustrate the effects of size and diversity. Some are more labour intensive than others and more suitable for small quantities of the product. For others the reverse is true.

Where the firm's products do not each pass through all of the possible manufacturing subsections and/or where they make differing demands upon the subsections, then the cost of these separate processes *must* be ascertained. An assembly is unlikely to be welded and soldered. It will be one or the other.

The variety of equipment suggested in the above operations will surely involve plant of widely differing initial purchase costs. They will also have varying running costs and even varying floor area space within the whole factory. Some may even require special floors.

Cost and budget centres

For these reasons the total overhead (see Exhibit 3.1 as an example) needs to be allocated to cost groupings, for separate allocation to products, in our drive to ascertain the 'added' costs to be brought into the total manufacturing cost of the products which use the services provided by the factory.

Here we come to two new and important costing terms: 'cost centres', and 'budget centres'.

These definitions can be interpreted, broadly, as the division of a business into operations or activities where the impact of costs incurred and budgeted cost growth can be readily identified and budgeted. The former deals with the past, the latter with the future.

Factors which will have relevance in the allocation of overhead costs to these centres include:

Floor area occupancy by separate processes or activities The principle involved in allocating rent and rates of buildings; expenses of maintaining buildings; cost of lighting where subsections each require similar lighting; heating and cleaning costs (though a cubic capacity method may be a more realistic criterion for heating and some warehousing).

Value of machine and equipment Depreciation of plant, its maintenance and any related running costs.

These guidelines for the allocation of the overhead costs to units of output or products should show the manager how to arrive at the specific costs of the different operations. If we can identify (as we ought to) a section or department where a *manager can be accorded responsibility* for cost control, then we have not just a cost collecting centre but a budgetary control centre also. The latter defines an area of *responsibility* for budgetary control, as well as for the aggregation of costs.

The entire premises may be the budget centre, especially in smaller businesses. Nevertheless we shall find that often there may be cost centres as well as subsidary budget centres. They each play their part in *cost* identification of processes, and control of activity expenditure within a *budget*.

Exhibit 3.2 below gives some extra detail to Exhibit 3.1 in that it specifies the stages in an overall fixed cost allocation in the pricing structure of a firm's (various) units of output.

Exhibit 3.2 *Pricing strategy*

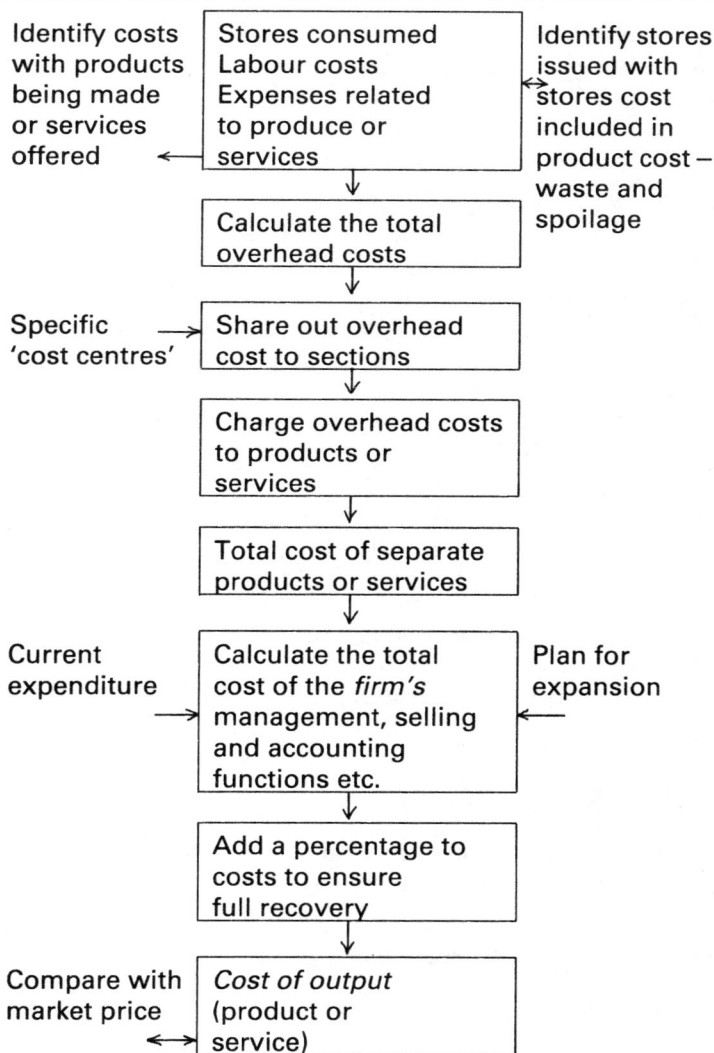

Identify costs with products being made or services offered	Stores consumed Labour costs Expenses related to produce or services	Identify stores issued with stores cost included in product cost – waste and spoilage

↓

Calculate the total overhead costs

↓

Specific 'cost centres' → Share out overhead cost to sections

↓

Charge overhead costs to products or services

↓

Total cost of separate products or services

↓

Current expenditure →	Calculate the total cost of the *firm's* management, selling and accounting functions etc.	← Plan for expansion

↓

Add a percentage to costs to ensure full recovery

↓

Compare with market price ↔ *Cost of output* (product or service)

4 Cost accounting II

We now proceed to use our knowledge of cost types and the ultimate allocation of their values to products being prepared for sale. The term 'product' changes its meaning with its context and is used extensively in many different businesses because it is specifically the result of labour.

If we were pedantic only the word 'artefact' would be used to describe the output from a manufacturing business. In another context the financial services use 'product' to describe the various schemes which they offer to potential investors! As it is familiar to both the manufacturing and service sectors it is used in this chapter.

Here the varying impacts of variable and overhead costs upon a firm's profitability can be shown with greatest effect in a break-even chart (see Glossary). Now the term 'break-even' specifies that level of output where the total cost of the firm's output of goods or service is equal to the total sales income from that output.

For the purpose of our initial break-even studies, we shall assume that a proposed selling price and the expected variable costs of a single product have been established and that the relationships are linear. A sum of fixed costs which the single product must cover, on the road to profitability, will also be given. The application of this exercise to a multi-product firm does not create great problems, as we shall subsequently see.

Product cost and break-even point

Example A

The following cost data refers to the smaller business being engaged in the sale of a sole product. Furthermore the maximum output is deemed to be 800 units.

	£
Expected selling price per unit	100
Variable cost per unit	35
Total fixed costs	26,000

A comparison of the inescapable variable costs with the unit's expected selling price shows a 'surplus' of £65. This so-called surplus indicates that sum, gained from the sale of one item, which is available to meet the fixed costs of the business. At this point we can specify the firm's break-even point from the following formula where the 'surplus' is now defined more realistically as the product's *contribution* to meeting total fixed costs.

$$\frac{\text{total fixed costs}}{\text{contribution per unit}} = \text{break-even output level}$$

$$= \frac{26,000}{65}$$

$$= 400 \text{ units of output at break-even}$$

A simple trading account will show the proof of the forecast break-even point.

	£	£
Sales income: 400 units at £100		40,000
Variable costs: 400 units at £35 per unit	14,000	
Total fixed costs	26,000	
Total costs		40,000
Profit or loss		nil

Exhibit 4.1 shows a conventional break-even chart in respect of the anticipated costs and income of the smaller company's product. At the foot of the chart, costs and incomes are tabulated to facilitate the reader's ready appreciation of that chart.

There are, however, warnings to be noted in the way a break-even chart is used. It does not intend (as may appear from Exhibit 4.1) to suggest a permanent cost/income relationship. To achieve such an ever growing sales and output relationship would most likely require some special efforts to be made. These efforts could include:

1   A sales campaign in existing territories or a move into new
    markets.
2   Improvements in methods, premises and equipment.
3   Changes to the payment system for employees.

See Exhibit 4.2 below.
Clearly such policies will involve additional costs, giving a

Exhibit 4.1 *Break-even chart*

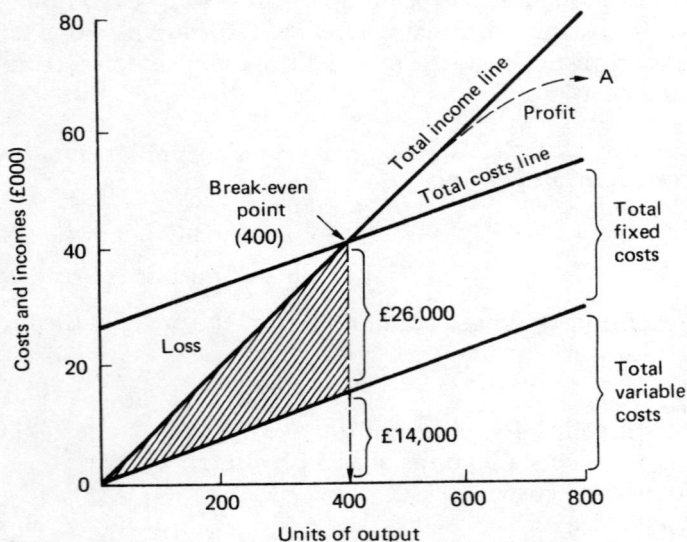

Table of costs/incomes

Sales in units	Variable costs	Fixed costs	Total costs	Sales income	Profit (+) or loss (−)
	£	£	£	£	£
200	7,000	26,000	33,000	20,000	−13,000
400	14,000	26,000	40,000	40,000	Break-even
600	21,000	26,000	47,000	60,000	+13,000
800	28,000	26,000	54,000	80,000	+26,000

marked impact upon the net returns gained from sales. No doubt their need would be most evident at the higher ranges of output and sales. Therefore the chart in Exhibit 4.1 includes a possible deviation in the total income line; the dotted line suggests a new direction of total income to point A at maximum output.

This is not to reject the principle of break–even: it is still an important factor to consider because management must be aware of the outputs needed for the business to pass from operating losses to net profits.

Planning ratios

At this stage we introduce two useful control ratios which will assist the business manager in forward planning.

These ratios are:

1 The margin of safety.
2 The profit/volume ratio.

Margin of safety

The amount of the total expected output which sits above the break–even point is termed the margin of safety. It describes the amount by which output could fall before the business enters the loss making area. It is exemplified in the formula★:

$$\frac{\text{number of output units above break-even point}}{\text{number of output units at maximum output}} \times 100 = \frac{400}{800} \times 100 = 50\%$$

A margin of safety of 50% tells us that output could fall by 50% before the firm begins to suffer losses. Clearly it is beneficial to have as wide a margin of safety as possible in order to combat any unfavourable problems of manufacture, or which may stem from a general trade recession. Finally, the reader should remember that any emergent variations in the variable cost per unit of product, contribution per unit of product and total fixed costs will react upon the margin of safety percentage rating.

★ Using the data quoted in paragraph 1 of Example A.

Profit/volume ratio

If we calculate the product's contribution as a percentage of its expected selling price, we arrive at the profit/volume ratio of:

$$\frac{\text{contribution per unit}}{\text{selling price per unit}} \times 100 = \frac{65}{100} \times 100 = 65\%$$

Here we have a percentage rating which specifies the proportion of sales income which will add to a business's profit *when the break-even point has been achieved*. This can be of significant value in a multi-product firm when changes in packages of output are being considered.

Accepting the data given in Exhibit 4.1 we can test the profit/volume ratio throughout the range of outputs shown in the chart and its accompanying table.

Sales in units	Total contribution at £65 per unit £	Income at £100 per unit £
400	26,000	40,000
600	39,000	60,000
800	52,000	80,000

The reader will find that the profit/volume ratio is confirmed at 65%. However, if the total income at the top of the sales range falls to £70,000 (see point A in the break-even chart) then the ratio will fall also.

Sales at the top of the range may be attained only at some extra cost, as explained on page 47. If we now accept the total sales income stemming from sales of 800 units to be £70,000 not £80,000, then clearly the net returns to the smaller business has fallen because either

1   The selling price has been reduced, or
2   Some of the costs of the operation have increased.

To sell 800 units for £70,000 suggests a price of:

$$\frac{£70,000}{800} = £87.5 \text{ per unit}$$

This would give a contribution of £52.5, if the variable costs

Exhibit 4.2 *Contribution growth*

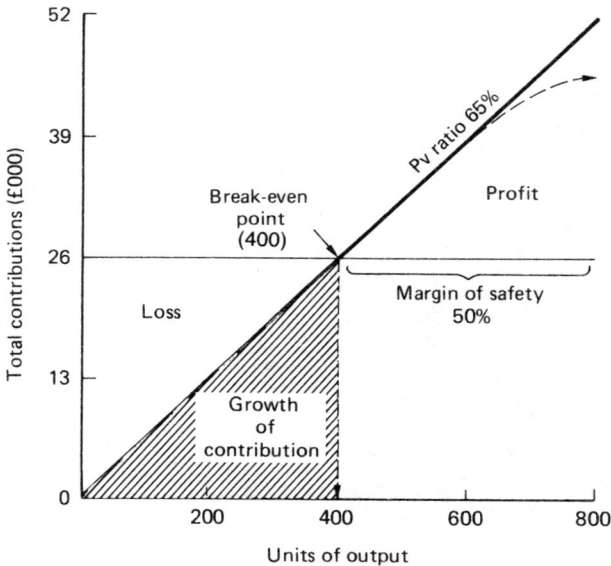

of £35 remained stable. The calculation of the products' profit/volume ratio will emphasize the changed circumstances

$$\frac{\text{contribution per unit} \times 100}{\text{selling price per unit}} = \frac{52.5}{87.5} \times 100 = 60\%$$

Conclusions

Exhibit 4.2 shows the relationship between the profit/volume ratio and the margin of safety, where total contributions, contributions per unit and the selling price per unit are taken to be as given in the immediately previous pages.

Clearly if the total recoverable overheads falls, then with the same profit volume ratio, the margin of safety will rise. This state of affairs would result from the lower break-even point which the reduced total sum of recoverable overheads would enable. Nevertheless it would not necessarily follow that, with the reduced overheads the manager would for ever

Exhibit 4.3 *Alternative strategies*

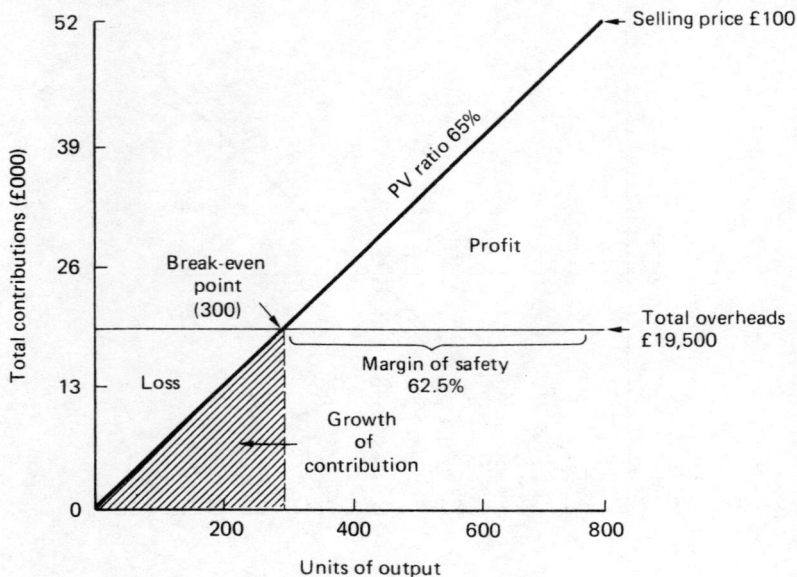

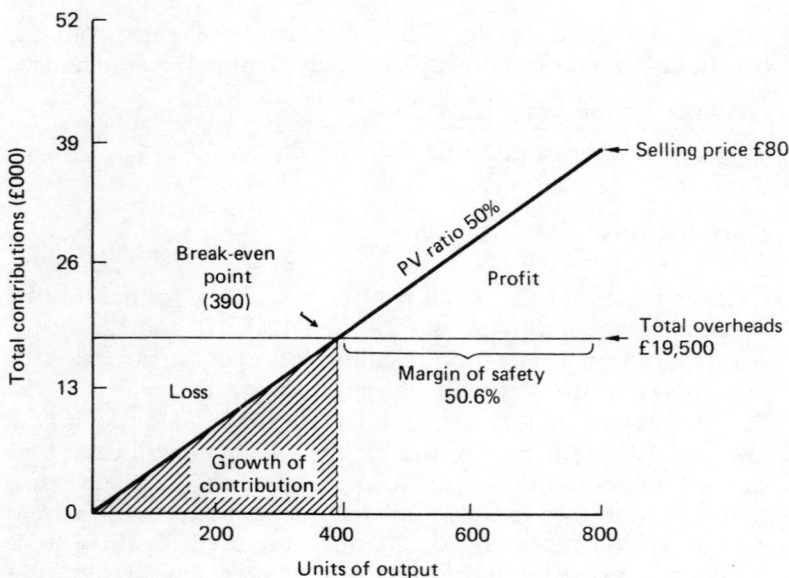

maintain a selling price of £100, for example. A reduction in selling price, with the same variable costs per unit, would then reduce the profit/volume ratio, raise the break-even point and establish a new margin of safety.

The reader should now recall the earlier break-even diagram shown in Exhibit 4.1 and the accompanying strictures against forming a rigid appreciation of the prospects offered by the conventional break-even chart (page 45). These strictures also apply to the diagrams shown in Exhibits 4.2 and 4.3. Then the vital relationship existing between the profit/volume ratio and the margin of safety concept, if viewed with care, will always guide the manager's ambitions for expansion or for taking over some other firm(s). Further advice on business development – by expansion or take-over follows in Chapter 14.

5 Cash flow

We turn our attention now to the firm's cash flow – probably one of the most important aspects in the survival and management of any business. Moreover, its importance for the smaller, sole proprietor form of trading enterprise, cannot be over-emphasized.

The term 'cash flow' is defined as the net cash being generated by a firm as a result of its trading activities. It primarily describes the flow of cash into and out of the business.

When cash income from sales and the return on investments *exceeds* its cash outflows resulting from its use of the various services (of labour, materials, overheads, etc.) necessary for its production and sales activities it is positive.

When outflows exceed inflows it is negative (see Exhibit 9.3).

The elements of cash flow

Many small business managers are principally concerned with today's cash position and that in the next few days and weeks. This is illustrated in Exhibit 9.8. That is raw cash flow.

Chapter 6 on financial control systems and Chapter 11 on credit management are particularly relevant to the control of raw cash flow.

As cash flow is also important in the medium term its definition has been refined and related to specific periods.

This chapter concentrates on refined cash flow. In order to determine the business's cash flow during a specified period, we shall – at first – use the data given in a profit and loss account. In these calculations we have to recognize that certain of the 'expenses' shown in profit and loss accounts do not

involve equal movements of cash. Depreciation is the most common example of a non-cash flow expense. The charge for depreciation represents the shared out portion of the cost of such fixed assets as *buildings, plant, machinery and vehicles* which are expected to have long lives. These facilities are expected to contribute to the operating activities of a business in the years during which such assets are available for use in the *producing, storing, marketing and distributing* of the products and services. The amount of a year's depreciation charge (shown in a profit and loss account) results in the reduction of the values of the related assets shown in the balance sheet. This asset value reduction will be coupled with the corresponding charge shown in the profit and loss account as an 'expense' (or cost) incurred in the securing of the sales income.

Example

A simple example will show how the profit and loss account data may be used to calculate a firm's cash flow. The account given below will enable the reader to test his or her assessments of cash flow at this *elementary stage* of learning about cash flow appraisal.

If we assume that the simplified account, shown below, related to a business where all the transactions were carried out in cash, then the period's cash flow generated by trading activities would be £3,200.

Exhibit 5.1 *Cash flow*

	£		£
Expenditure	4,000	Sales	8,000
Depreciation	800		
Profit before tax			
carried down	3,200		
	£8,000		£8,000
Taxation	800	Profit before	
Profit after tax	2,400	tax brought down	3,200
	£3,200		£3,200

$$\text{cash flow} = \text{sales} - (\text{expenditure} + \text{taxation})$$
$$= \pounds 8,000 - (4,000 + 800)$$
$$= \pounds 3,200$$

However, business activity and the settlement of accounts are conducted mostly on credit. Therefore some part of the sales income, shown in the profit and loss account, would be received in the subsequent accounting period. At the same time there will be a time lag in the payments for certain expenditures, again as a result of the operation of customary credit practices. But these comments can be made about the previous period's cash movements and therefore *it may be reasonably* acceptable to define cash flow as:

cash flow = profit after tax + the year's depreciation charges which Exhibit 5.1 will show as:

$$\text{cash flow} = \pounds 2,400 + 800$$
$$= \pounds 3,200$$

This agrees with our earlier calculation.

Further considerations

Our calculations of corporate cash flow have started with the sum of profits after tax. It is essential here to stress that the taxation sum in a profit and loss account will not yet have been paid – it will not become due for several months yet but it must not be overlooked in the face of more immediate needs. Clearly the taxation sum *paid* during the year in question is a more relevant factor to take into account in assessing a business's cash flow. Thus we may give a better view of an annual cash flow if we operate the following formula:

cash flow = profit before tax + the year's depreciation charges *minus* the taxation sum due shown in the previous year's accounts.

A practical approach

The foregoing calculations of a business's cash flows really

Exhibit 5.2 *The patterns of cash flows*

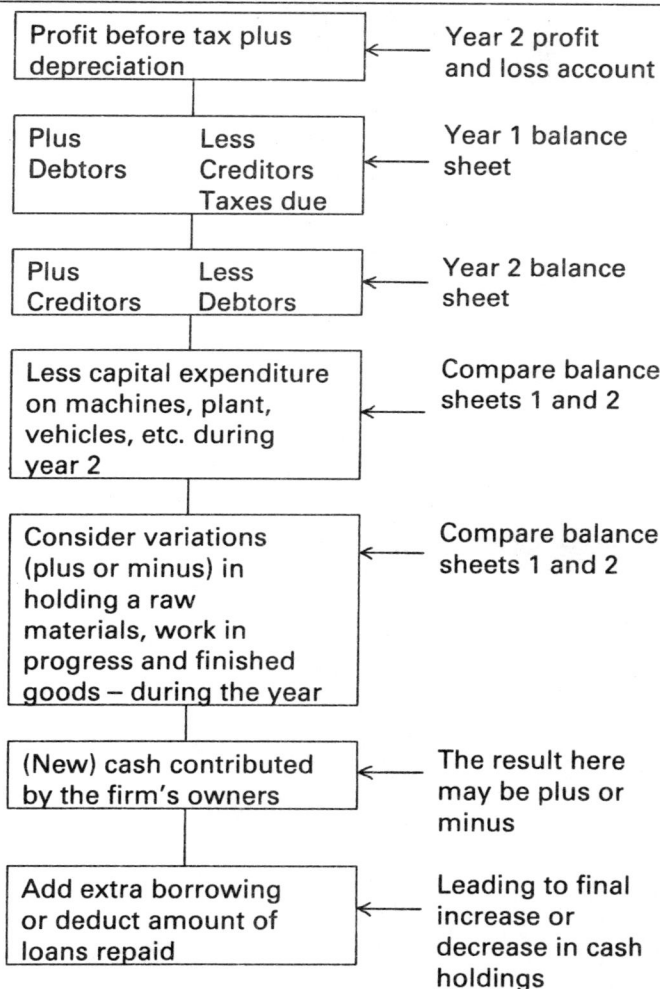

Profit before tax plus depreciation	Year 2 profit and loss account
Plus · · · · · Less Debtors · · · Creditors · · · · · · · · · Taxes due	Year 1 balance sheet
Plus · · · · · Less Creditors · · Debtors	Year 2 balance sheet
Less capital expenditure on machines, plant, vehicles, etc. during year 2	Compare balance sheets 1 and 2
Consider variations (plus or minus) in holding a raw materials, work in progress and finished goods – during the year	Compare balance sheets 1 and 2
(New) cash contributed by the firm's owners	The result here may be plus or minus
Add extra borrowing or deduct amount of loans repaid	Leading to final increase or decrease in cash holdings

express the hoped for stream of cash in–flows, generated by its trading operations – if all goes according to plan. Each of our formulae for the quantification of a corporate cash flow has involved the data in a profit and loss account. Yet it has been clearly stated (page 20) that the profit and loss account does not measure movements of cash: it deals with comparisons of *expenditure with incomes, not* the results arising from comparisons of *payments with receipts* which will always be found in the cash book and/or the bank's statements of account.

Therefore, while our earlier examples have quite properly been devoted to the accounting definitions of cash flow the fact is that it has merely indicated the flow of cash which *ought to flow in* from the business's operations. Such corporate cash flow statements are of considerable value in:

- Comparing one business with another when the accounts are available.
- Charting progress from year to year.
- Considering the worthwhileness of business expansions (see Chapter 8).
- Assessing the need for additional permanent capital for such expansions or developments.

So we may look at a most important factor in cash flow analysis when we start to examine our own business's affairs, and to compare its effectiveness with that of other firms. If the manager aims at expansion, and is looking for such further growth by taking over some other concern(s) then he or she must obtain, and study, the final accounts of the desired takeover unit or units. Exhibit 5.2 indicates how the cash flow problem can be identified when *two years'* final accounts are available for analysis.

6   Financial control systems

A sole proprietor can have the same problems or organizational security as a larger firm. He or she still needs to safeguard assets from fraud and theft (see Exhibits 1.1–1.4) as does every other business. Now a control of assets – particularly money and money's worth – can be greatly aided by the establishment of the firm's own audit section. Internal audit, (see Glossary) involves a group of the firm's employees who are continually engaged in independent* verifications of the business's transactions and the stewardship of its assets. However, it is not suggested here that every small business must immediately establish such a staff section. Nevertheless, some of the generally accepted principles and practices of financial control should be well understood by the smallest business operators. Relevant computer programs are listed in Part Five, Appendix 1.

Internal control

The definition of internal control (see Glossary) implies that the daily transactions of the business, should be regularly and continuously checked either manually or by computer . It does not always suggest that each single transaction is noted and verified in the books of account. Although till rolls and the issuing of receipts to VAT registered customers often makes this possible. It does require, however, that the work of one person is tested independently by the work of some other person(s). This *checking* system can be effected by the

---

* Independent of the staff who are employed in the day-to-day recording of individual transactions – be it of cash or goods movement etc. – and keeping the various ledgers and records.

matching of independently produced total sums against the relevant individual entries in the firm's ledgers. Examples of this practice, given below, will show how some automatic procedures can achieve a measure of security in the records of the affairs of the business:

1   Total cash received and banked each day should be matched with the bank's statement of account, the cash book, and against the copy sales invoices to which the receipts relate.

2   A cashier responsible for receiving cash should not have any duties relating to the sales ledger account wherein the debtors' sums due are recorded.

3   Each day's postings to the sales ledger accounts should be automatically summarized at the time of posting, by the ledger clerk or machine operator, and independently agreed with the relevant totals shown each day in the cash book. Frequent comparisons of cheques listed in bank paying-in slips should be made with the related named accounts in the books of account. This action will ensure that:

(a)   The correct debtor's account is credited with those payments by cheque.

(b)   An outstanding account for which a cash payment is received was not fraudulently credited with the value of a banked cheque or draft whilst the related cash was misappropriated (see control of receipt forms below).

The operation listed in (b) above can be developed so that cash items can be stolen, where cash book and debtor accounts are kept by the same person, or where collusion exists between two individuals. The cash payer's accounts will be subsequently credited, irregularly, with other cheques, in order to defer the debtors' enquiries about the amounts shown as outstanding in, e.g. their monthly notices of sums due.

The *banking* of cash receipts should normally be accomplished daily. In this operation it is advisable that:

(c)   Visits to the bank should be to its nearest branch and at irregular times during the day.

(d)   The timing of each banking should be decided by the manager or senior cashier – without prior notice to the rest of the staff.

(e) Similarly, where substantial sums are being trans-
ported, different routes to the bank should be specified – from day to day – by the manager.

Cash control

Cash, money orders, drafts and cheques will be received over
the counter or by post. They may be addressed to a Post Office
box number which is allocated to the business. The persons
responsible must obey the following procedures:

1 Ensure that every cheque and money order is crossed for
payment to the firm's bank, with the instruction 'to
account payee only': correctly signed, not post-dated, and
that words and figures agree.
2 Each postal receipt should be immediately recorded in a
register of monies received by post. Two individuals
should certify the completeness and accuracy of each day's
operations.
3 Postal receipts may then be handed to the cashier, or the
manager, for depositing in the bank and recording in the
cash book. The recipient of the cash (cashier or manager)
should sign the postal receipts register evidencing responsibility for those items. The cashier, or the manager alone
will have the authority for issuing receipts for monies
received.

Clearly the supply of receipt documents, whether in
booklet form or as separate documents, should be serially
numbered and retained under the control of the manager.

External payments

Similarly cheque books, used for making payments in settlement of various accounts owing by the business or in advance
when credit terms are not available must be safely secured in
the possession of the manager. Some managers keep them at
home. We also emphasize that the manager – or an authorized
representative – should sign cheques or other negotiable
instruments (see Glossary) only after comparison with specific

evidence of the amounts due to be paid to a supplier or other form of creditor. Extra care is needed with direct debit authorizations. Many small businesses mandate their banks to accept only the manager's signature although this can cause problems in the event of a prolonged absence from the office.

The practice of signing a number of blank cheques, for a subordinate employee to utilize in the settlement of claims from creditors of other known suppliers, must be completely rejected. It may save the manager's time but could result in theft or misuse of the firm's cash by that subordinate.

Payments made by cash should be supported by a receipt from the supplier.

All payments should be made when they become due and neither before nor after.

Cash documents security

The security of cash receipts necessitates reference to safe-box or strongroom facilities for the retention – perhaps only overnight or maybe for longer periods – of cash, cheques, deeds, documents and other contracts relating to the firm's activities and its assets. Where strongroom facilities are used for cash *and* documents storage then access to the contents thereof should:

1   Involve two persons, each holding one of the two keys★ necessary to open the safe or strongroom door.
2   A register should be kept of each document placed in the safe or vault, and of items removed therefrom. Each entry in the register should be signed by the two key holders, evidencing their supervision of the individual deposits or removals.

The strongroom type of document and cash security may not be available for the smaller type of business. Nevertheless a safe storage facility is necessary for cash receipts, cheque

★ Where access to safe or strongroom is achieved by combination locks, the whole combination should either (1) be in the possession of the manager only, or (2) two persons should each possess one part of the combination code necessary to gain access to the safe or strongroom.

books and receipt forms. For these purposes the following safeguards are recommended:

1 The safe-box should be encased in concrete so it cannot be easily removed and forcibly entered once off the site.
2 Sink the safe-box in the floor, again surrounding it in concrete, with its opening activated by the two-key system.

Even with the single safe-box facility it is advised that the two-key system should be operated.

Payments verification

The security of cash receipts and other relevant documents is but one aspect of controlling the firm's liquid cash resources and, incidentally, the size of its bank overdraft. Therefore we now examine the systems for verification and control of *payments* made by the business for its supplies of goods and services.* Again the separation of duties between various staff members should be evident from the application of the following stages in a stock control system:

1 Orders for goods and services must be initiated only by the manager or an authorized individual manager. Store-keepers should not have the authority to order goods, whether of raw materials, plant or machinery etc. Their duties will require them to conduct regular verifications of the quantities of stock items held. So they should be able to advise the manager of any emerging needs due to falling stock levels, when the manager will decide, from a knowledge of programmes of work, whether to initiate restocking orders.
2 All goods received must be accompanied by a delivery note. The quantities, satisfactory condition and types of the goods should be verified by the storekeeper – *at the time of receipt* – against the information on the delivery note *and* against a copy of the official order issued by the business.

---

* Here our attention will not be limited to supplies of raw materials and components. *All* goods received including plant, machinery and related spare parts must be subject to the same scrutiny control and safe storage.

3 Stores receipts accepted in accordance with the above rules should be forthwith recorded on stores records (e.g. bin cards), and placed in secure storage places to avoid theft and/or deterioration through unsatisfactory, damp or insecure, open situations.

4 The issue of goods from the storehouse should be authorized by an issue note signed by the manager or an authorized signatory. Personnel then taking goods from the store must sign a goods issue note detailing the items taken.

   Such issues must also be recorded on the relevant bin card(s).

5 Ledger accounts should be kept, for each storehouse section, showing the value of stores in hand. It is not expected that each separate group of stock items will be recorded in this way, though it would facilitate 'spot checks' (by internal audit or senior manager) taken with the object of agreeing the stores values held with the recorded ledger values.

   Whichever system is operated the ledger totals recording stock values, should be verified against the actual total value of stocks held.

6 A regular system of verifying selected bin card totals with the physical stocks held in the appropriate storage, should be in force. Any discrepancies must be reported to the manager and be investigated. It is in such matters that the security of the storehouse may need reviewing.

Returnable containers

Controls over containers, in which goods are received by the firm *and* which the firm may use in the despatch of its own products to customers, should be established. Records must be kept

1 By the storekeeper of containers relating to goods received and for which a charge may be made. The record should:
   (a) Detail the number and type of each container received and its storage site.
   (b) Show the date of return of the containers and the number of the goods returned document.

2   All sales invoices for the firm's own products should specify separately the type and value of the containers used. The despatch department should keep a record of such containers issued. Non-return of the containers after allowing a specified period (one month) should be notified to the manager for an appropriate charge invoice to be issued to the customer.

Wages and salary payments

Here again systems of control over cash payments demand the operation of a minimum of internal check procedures. The division of duties between sections of staff can provide a measure of security against the falsification of wage and salary payments. Clearly the main objective must be to avoid:

1   The insertion of false names in wage and salary sheets, and the misappropriation (theft) of the related sums shown as payable.
2   Inflation of wage and salary sheet totals resulting in cash drawn from the bank – for wage and salary payments – in excess of that sum properly calculated and required; the excess amount being stolen.

The system of internal check aims for the division of duties between staff so that, apart from an improper collusion between two or more employees, it becomes an essential safeguard against misappropriation of the firm's cash. 'Forgery' and 'fraud' are defined in the Glossary. It is imperative therefore that the actual operation of the system is verified by frequent test checks carried out by the internal audit section – if one exists – or by the manager or a representative.

Any system is effective *only if it is regularly and properly operated*. Therefore the frequent verification of that fact is equally essential.

Internal check system

Details of an acceptable internal check system are given below.

Its various operations, which are shown as being allotted to different groups of the firm's staff, may seem more appropriate to companies large enough to have sufficient employees to enable such separate staff sections to be identified. Nevertheless, the manager of the smallest business should examine the suggested system in order to appreciate the need for separation of duties. He or she should consider how well he or she can achieve the safeguards implicit in the procedures now outlined:

1 The authority to employ and pay any individual must be authorized by a note, issued by a manager, to the wage and salary section.
2 The preparation of wages and salaries due, each week or month, evidenced by time cards and employment note, should be completed in the wage and salary section: a summary of the totals of each payments sheet should be also completed in that section.
3 Collection of cash from the bank – cheques for this purpose to be signed by the manager and agreed with the above summary sheet – by staff employed in the preparation of wage packets or the preparation of cheques for 'non-cash' payees.*
4 When issuing wage packets, the signature of the payee must be obtained and the payee must be identified by a witness (e.g. foreman) who also signs the paysheet.
5 Unpaid wages should be returned to the manager or cashier and immediately entered in the 'unclaimed wages' book: the entry in this book must be signed by the payee when subsequently paid, after presenting adequate identification. Instances of repeated unpaid wages for a named payee should be reported to the manager for investigation.

Conclusions

The foregoing examples of internal control systems, which operate to safeguard the firm against loss, should now lead the manager of even the smallest firm to consider the working

---

* Note carefully here – the staff who prepare the wage and salary sheets must be excluded from this operation.

practices operating in his or her own domain. It is essential to realize that loss can arise through:

1 Fraud – the theft or misappropriation of cash or other documents of a monetary value.
2 Theft or misuse of the firm's assets – raw material stocks, finished goods, office equipment, manufacturing plant and loose tools.
3 Fraudulent manipulation of the firm's account books in order to conceal the true position regarding the firm's assets and its profitability.

The business manager should ensure that – at least – those who receive and otherwise handle cash, postal orders, cheques and other negotiable instruments should never be concerned with:

1 The preparation of any of the related ledger accounts, wage and salary payments or any accounts detailing the firm's assets.
2 Authorizing payments to creditors or preparing the related accounts; controlling the stock of cheques, receipt or invoice documents (all of which should be serially numbered and retained under the direct control of the manager).
3 Personnel who will use raw materials, equipment or other assets should have no authority to order new supplies, arrange their storage, or authorize their issue from the storehouse.

7 Budgeting

An earlier section of this book referred to cost centres and budget centres. We now re-emphasize their appropriateness to budgetary control. The two terms are epitomized as follows:

1 The cost centre is a regular systematic collection of costs for specific segments of the business or for defined operating functions. In each of these circumstances a senior member of the firm should be responsible both for the section's/area's management and its achievement of output cost targets.
2 The budget centre is defined as a division or section of the firm where approved budgetary expense limits should be controlled and the progress reported. It may also be a centre where product development and innovation may arise, where management are involved in setting future output targets and thus playing some part in the plan of action for the next operating period.

Chapter 10 shows that budgeting differs from financial planning (see page 99).

The terms budget, budget variance, capital budgeting, cash budget, flexible budget and forecast are defined in the Glossary.

The budget process

Satisfactory budgets are not achieved by taking the current year's costs and outputs and varying them by set percentages which the manager, e.g., thinks is most appropriate to the future period. Increasing the year's costs, output and expected profits by 5% or 10% or some other arbitrary view, does not describe a sound budgeting exercise.

Budgeting may be compared to cutting the coat according to the cloth. It involves dividing what is available into a number of unequal, essential parts which have to be fitted together.

What is available for division into parts is the income of the business from sales. The parts are the different budget centres, departments and sections of the business which have their own sometimes conflicting needs for money (see Chapter 10, page 109).

The foundation of any budget is a framework of quantifiable relationships between the different budget centres. These may change when a more up-to-date statement of expected income or demands for resources becomes available.

These relationships can be easily expressed as simple equations. If the budget for the whole business equals 100, marketing may be allocated 20%. This could be subdivided into advertising + exhibitions + sales force + storage + distribution. Each could be allocated an equal 4% of the marketing budget to give $4 + 4 + 4 + 4 + 4 = 20\%$, or some other basis used such as $4 + 1 + 8 + 2 + 5 = 20\%$. Other cost information may be incorporated into equations where it is available. If it is not projections will be necessary.

The availability of personal computers with spreadsheet (see Glossary) facilities has made the manipulation of these relationships and the portrayal of the effects of different levels of activity much easier than it was in the past. As it is possible to waste time on too many iterations three levels of sales activity are suggested in this chapter. These are manageable whether the budget preparation is manual or computerized.

Three levels of a budget

A budget which is based upon *one expected level* of sales, will have consequences for:

- The overall cost per unit of a product or service
- Labour requirement (type of skills required)
- Premises and facilities
- Purchase programme for goods and services
- Other operating expenses e.g. packaging

- Equipment repair and replacement
- Adequate financing arrangements from internal or external sources.

Clearly it is unlikely in a small business that the budget for one level of activity will be able to deal with all future, unforeseen, variations in the business climate as it affects each of the above areas. Sales forecasting is too difficult for that to be a possibility.

The reader will be aware from Chapter 4 of the effect of variations in output upon product costs. The allocation of overheads, determination of costs per unit, will all change with variations in output. Therefore any comparisons of future actual costs against the data in a single-level budget, will result in the lack of comparisons of 'like with like'. Erroneous conclusions for cost variations and other related business shortcomings could result in wrong operating decisions being taken.

We shall therefore suggest an approach which envisages that each year's budget should be expressed in three levels of potential activity. It has to be recognized that, in most successful businesses, sales forecasts are rarely specified at one single level. A range of possible achievements is given, when all the problems arising from variations in business activity can be seen. Their impact on the several areas of the firm's operations can be defined and realistically interpreted.

It is here that the potential of the departmental managers, who control the cost/budget centres, will be seen at its most effective. They will be required to give their statements of resources requirements consequent upon each of the three proposed budget levels. It is essential that the maker of the budget should meet with departmental managers, in order to inform them of their required contributions to and expectations from the overall budget.

First proposed level of operations – the basic minimum

At this stage the manager should consider the lowest level of activity which a centre needs to make use of the resources it has at present. He or she must also consider the minimum levels of resources which are essential to the effective continuance of the unit. Here we have some cost reduction implications when the total resources available to the unit are to be established at lower output levels. Detailed cost and other financial analyses will accompany the budget.

Second proposed level of operations – maintaining current levels

Now the manager, accepting the present level of activity, needs to specify the resources – plant, labour, stores, finance, etc. – which he or she will need, over and above those recorded at the plan expressed in the first budget. He or she will detail those resources which a centre must continue to have, in good working order, with replacements envisaged where necessary, in order to maintain its present contributions to the firm's outputs, at a cost-effective status.

Third proposed level of operations – expansion

We now come to the point where an expansion of the present output is to be considered. Again the resources needed will be expected to be over and above those specified for the second budget stage. It will show how the extra efforts, implicit in the third budget can be achieved. Important features will include the *new* resources required at the budget centre in order to obtain the higher level of output which it proposes. The evaluation of the worthwhileness of capital expenditure (see Chapter 8) will be the responsibility of the manager who will budget for *the management of the business* at the various levels of operation *and* the related requirements for finance.

Conclusions

Benefits to the firm's management style cannot fail but accrue from the foregoing exercises in budgeting. The manager will have a wider picture of the consequences which may develop from several development programmes. A preferential ordering of any (increased?) expenditure proposals, which emerge from the three future plans, can be established. But any past practices of starting a 'next-year' budget with today's cost/output data, and their variation by assumed percentage increases, or decreases, will be defeated. Future projections of costs/outputs will be the more securely based.

The programme which is ultimately accepted will be strengthened by cost/budget benefits promised by individual managers. Future comparisons of actual costs with the budgeted output costs, will be more realistically based. Nevertheless it has to be stressed that the final decisions, on a specific budget plan, will be made by the manager in consultation with various departmental and budget centre managers who may not necessarily agree with or like the decisions.

Clearly if a 'growing-in-trading' approach is accepted as the basic element in the emergent plan, the manager must give attention to problems arising out of:

1   Overtrading, i.e., expanding output without having parallel plans for secure cash flows, or providing new capital funds. The cost of new finance may represent a greater risk than the business can bear.
2   Borrowing threshold, i.e., the limits beyond which further borrowings may be considered unwise. It is suggested that the threshold is passed where (a) total borrowing exceeds the manager's invested funds, and (b) where interest payments absorb more than 50% of pre-tax profits.
3   Staffing levels, i.e., growth may require extra managerial specialist staffs. It must form part of the budget for future periods.

8 Investment appraisal

Chapters 2, 3 and 4 were concerned with reporting and appraising the *past performance* of businesses: ROCE, return on sales, turnover of capital employed, the analysis of working capital and its constituent stocks, debtors and creditors. Each of these factors had given a view of the effectiveness of the firm's management and use of the assets.

There is a major change of emphasis as in Chapter 7 which deals with budgeting for future business developments. In that chapter it was shown that departmental managers could be required to look into the future and assess the firm's power to expand or, perhaps, to reduce its existing level of operations. The three budget plans proposed in Chapter 7 suggest a need to consider future:

1 Work schedules and any consequent need for new plant, equipment and other assets.
2 Cash flows and the avoidance of insolvency.
3 Borrowing thresholds, and possible needs for adequate additional managerial staffs.

Project appraisal

We shall now examine in this chapter certain techniques for assessing the future benefits which are expected to accrue from new capital investment. Various sophisticated methods of investment appraisal are available, but we shall concentrate on the simplest, yet most appropriate for the smaller business, i.e. the 'cash-recovery' value of all new fixed asset expenditures. It will be most likely that many businesses cannot afford all of the suggested capital expenditure proposals, which emerge from the budgeting exercise. Therefore we must place the various recommended projects in some easily identifiable order of preference.

Payback

Here we have the 'cash-recovery' index of a project's value. As the cash benefits from capital expenditure are forecast to accrue, mostly, in future years, then the sooner the original capital outlay is recovered from future cash flows, the better it will be for the firm's liquidity state. The extent of the 'cash at risk period' is thus defined.

Exhibit 8.1 below suggests four different investment projects, detailing their capital costs and their related cash inflows in each of the five years of the projects' lives. The annual cash flows data assume that the yearly cash returns are received evenly throughout the year.

Exhibit 8.1 *Payback rating of competing investment projects*

Project	Capital cost in year0 £	Incremental cash flows in each year					Total cash flows £
		1 £	2 £	3 £	4 £	5 £	
A	20,000	5,000	5,000	5,000	5,000	5,000	25,000
B	20,000	1,000	3,000	6,000	7,000	8,000	25,000
C	30,000	8,000	8,000	8,000	8,000	8,000	40,000
D	20,000	2,000	4,000	6,000	8,000	10,000	30,000

Using the 'cash recovery' criterion of the worth of each investment to the business, we find the following payback indexes for each of the projects:

A   4 years (£5,000 per year for 4 years).
B   4⅜ years (£1,000 + £3,000 + £6,000 + £7,000 + ⅜ of £8,000).
C   3¾ years (£8,000 + £8,000 + £8,000 + ¾ of £8,000).
D   4 years (£2,000 + £4,000 + £6,000 + £8,000).

Therefore, from the standpoint of early recovery of the

initial cash outlay, the order of preference for choosing one of these projects would be:

1	*C*
2 and 3	*A* and *D*
4	*B*

The cost of money

Assessing a simple payback rating by reference to the whole of each year's expected future cash flows has one major defect. It fails to reflect the (per annum) cost of money. Clearly £5,000 to be received five years hence cannot have the same value attraction as £5,000 receivable in one year's time. Again the reader is referred to the essential validity of comparing 'like to like'. So we must adjust the several years' cash flows by that cost (of money) caused by the time delay in receipt of the cash relating to each passing year's values.

In this way our appraisal of the worth of alternative investments is accomplished in a more effective way by:

1 Reducing each year's forecast cash flows by a cost of money, i.e., a rate of interest or some other cost of capital to the firm – which is charged for *each year's delay* in receipt of the cash flow, so that
2 The total of the several years' discounted★ cash flows will represent the total value of the future cash flows which will be properly comparable with the initial capital outlay in year 0, the year of the project investment.

Discounting calculations

To calculate a future year's discounted cash flows we must turn to Part 5, Appendix 4 (page 196). There we have the discounting factors applicable at various interest rates for each of a series of years. Table 1, Appendix 4 gives the *present value* of a sum of £1 receivable in a future year, in respect of a series of interest rates quoted at the head of the table. If we assume the

★ 'Discounted' means reduced by a cost of money factor.

Exhibit 8.2 *Discounted yearly cash flows*

10% discount factor for each year	Each year's discounted cash flow					Totals
	1	2	3	4	5	
	0.9091	0.8264	0.7513	0.6830	0.6209	
Project Capital cost in year 0	£	£	£	£	£	£

	£						
A	20,000	4,546	4,132	3,757	3,415	3,104	18,954
B	20,000	1,909	2,479	4,508	4,781	4,967	17,644
C	30,000	7,273	6,611	6,010	5,464	4,967	30,325
D	20,000	1,818	3,306	4,508	5,464	6,209	21,305

firm's cost of capital to be 10%, then the 'reducing factors' to be applied to each £1 of income, receivable in each of the first five years of the project lives will be:

Year	Discounted cash flow
1	0.9091
2	0.8264
3	0.7513
4	0.6830
5	0.6209

The present value of £5,000, expected to be received in one year's time, becomes:

$$£5,000 \times 0.9091 = £4,546$$

Exhibit 8.2 now presents the expected cash flows from each of the alternative investment proposals, in a way truly comparable with the initial outlay cost. The new value accorded to the future cash return has taken account of the money cost of the delay in receipt of those forecast incomes. These new values are now properly comparable with the initial outlay on the related investment.

Conclusions

Immediately it is abundantly clear that projects A and B do not recover their initial outlay costs (including the cost of capital) in their specified five year periods. Therefore we must turn our attention to projects C and D.

Project C
The total of the discounted cash flows for years 1 to 4 amounts to £25,358, leaving £4,642 to be recovered from the income of year 5 in order to recover the whole of the project's outlay cost.

The required sum of £4,642 represents 93% of the fifth year's cash flows. The project's discounted payback is therefore 4.93 years!

Project D
Here, a summation of the first four years' discounted cash flows is shown to be £15,096, leaving £4,904 to be allocated from the fifth year's flows in order to recover the project's invested cost (plus the interest cost for the intervening years). As £4,904 is 79% of the final year flows of £6,209, the project's discounted payback is 4.79 years.

Both projects are marginally acceptable but project D has 'the edge' over project C. However its apparently favourable 'cash recovery' index depends upon its final year's *large* cash flows of £10,000, a forecast of its expected returns five years hence. Such a forecast into the distant future may contain *some* doubtful elements in it, which would then lead the manager of the firm to place both projects on an equal payback basis.

A final point about the discounting tables involves the use of Table 2 in Appendix 4. Here the interest factors give the present value of a *series* of £1 flows received in each year, for any series of years. Therefore, if undiscounted cash flows, in each of a series of years, are equal, then we need to make but one calculation only to arrive at the total discounted returns. In Table 2 the discounting factor at year 5 is 3.7908. If this is multiplied by the figure of each year's equal flows (£5,000) we have the total flows of £18,954. A similar calculation for project C will give the sum of £30,326 the marginal change from that total achieved by summation of each year's separate discounted cash flows, shown in Exhibit 8.2, being the result of rounding up the various indexing factors.

Net cash flows

The foregoing projects were relatively easy to evaluate. The examples were classified in an order of preferential acceptance – the 'cash recovery' or payback criterion. Furthermore the payback rating has been shown in the context of *discounted* cash flows. No change is being suggested here to our recommended use of the discounted payback index of investment choice.

However, evaluating a project's net cash flows is not as simple as may be displayed in Exhibits 8.1 and 8.2. Net cash flows must describe those cash flows which *remain with the company* as a result of the projected investment. So we must bring to our appraisals the *after-tax gains* stemming from a project, in order to reach a viable assessment of any project's worth.

This process will bring to the account any government grants or incentives which are made to encourage/assist firms to invest in, say, new plant and machinery. Such incentives have varied from time to time. Therefore, we shall demonstrate the post-tax impacts upon an investment's cash flows by applying the following principles, which do not represent any major variations from the existing practices:

1   The expected profits (i.e., gross cash flows) from an investment is deemed to bear tax in the year following the actual expenditure, at a rate of 25%.
2   Allowance against the *firm's* taxable liabilities shall be made on actual expenditure on, say, machinery and plant, at a rate of 25% of that expenditure.
3   The 25% is calculated on the reducing sum of the expenditure, after each year's 25% is deducted therefrom. This allowance is available for each *full* year that the equipment is retained. Where the equipment is installed halfway through the year, then the actual allowance against tax will be one half of the full year sum.

Exhibit 8.3 *Investment incentives (written down value allowances)*

Year	Cost and written down values	25% allowances on cost/ written down values	Tax saved by allowances	New year end written down value
(1)	*(2)* £	*(3)* £	*(4)* £	*(5)* £
1	20,000	5,000	1,250	15,000
2	15,000	3,750	938	11,250
3	11,250	2,812	703	8,438
4	8,438	2,110	527	6,328
5	6,328	1,582	395	4,746
6	4,746	4,746	1,187	—
		20,000	5,000	

Example

Project cost in year 0   £20,000
Gross cash flows in years 1 to 5   £8,000 per year

Exhibit 8.3 shows the taxes saved by the investment allowances in relation to each full year's value of the asset. This relates to an asset, initially costing £20,000 and having an expected life of five years. In year 1 we are shown the first year life values as:

	£
Initial cost	20,000
Full year's use: allowance at 25%	5,000
Company's written down book value at the end of year 1	15,000

The end of year 1 written down asset value of £15,000 then stands as the basis for the 25% tax allowance in year 2. Throughout the exhibit the effects of the investment allowance – against the firm's taxation liabilities – is shown in column 3. The calculation for year 1 is:

Investment allowance	£5,000
Taxation saved by this allowance, at 25%	£1,250

In the sixth year we assume that no disposable value, insurance or compensation money was received in the event of the asset's retirement. Should some monetary receipts arise, they would be offset against any written down value to assess whether:

1 Any taxation allowance is permissible.
2 Any taxation charge is to be levied if the receipts exceed the written down book value.

Exhibits 8.4 and 8.5 complete the appraisal of the proposed investment. Exhibit 8.4 shows the tax payable on each year's pre-tax profits *and* the taxes saved by the investment incentive scheme displayed in Exhibit 8.3.

Exhibit 8.4 *Net cash flows*

Year (1)	Profits before (2) £	Tax payable at 25% (3) £	Tax saved by investment allowances (4) £	Post-tax Net cash flows (5) £
1	8,000		1,250	9,250
2	8,000	(2,000)	938	6,938
3	8,000	(2,000)	703	6,703
4	8,000	(2,000)	527	6,527
5	8,000	(2,000)	395	6,395
6	—	(2,000)	1,187	(813)
	40,000	(10,000)	5,000	35,000

Finally, Exhibit 8.5 details, with the discounting, at our assumed 10% cost of money, to show true discounted net cash flows. The project is clearly acceptable and the discounted payback is 3.18 years.

Exhibit 8.5 *Discounted net cash flows*

Year (1)	Post tax net cash flows (2) £	10% discount factor (3)	Discounted net cash flows (4) £
1	9,250	0.9091	8,409
2	6,938	0.8264	5,734
3	6,703	0.7513	5,036
4	6,527	0.6830	4,458
5	6,395	0.6209	3,971
6	(813)	0.5645	(459)
	35,000		27,149

9 Presenting and illustrating financial information

The practice of using charts and diagrams to facilitate the rapid understanding of figures, although well established, is still gaining in popularity. Public companies print diagrams in their annual reports to shareholders. Newspapers and journals use them alongside their reports and comments. In small businesses they have great potential as an aid to communication and analysis especially in connection with business plans.

They have advantages for both the numerate and the non-numerate. Numerate personnel can grasp information more quickly than when presented only with figures and/or an associated text. Non-numerate personnel whose skills are not in financial management but elsewhere may grasp facts which would otherwise elude them. Financiers outside the business when pressed for time and preoccupied with the needs of larger businesses have the salient financial information presented succinctly.

Despite their advantages, diagrams have not and will not make tables and accounts obsolete because they have limitations as well as advantages. These are mentioned below when considering the merits and applications of the different types of diagrams. It is the advent of dry and adhesive-backed transfer materials, computer graphics (mono and coloured) and photocopying which has made it possible for small businesses to produce good quality diagrams without much skill in the graphic arts. Many photocopiers besides size for size copying can reduce and enlarge. Information can therefore be made available in an attractive manner to all interested parties who can work on it simultaneously. In fact precautions have to be taken to prevent too many copies being produced so that confidential information becomes available to those from whom it should be withheld!

Besides black-and-white photocopying there are colour

photocopiers. Whilst colour has advantages over black-and-white to give greater impact, these photocopiers are somewhat rare in small businesses. However black-and-white photocopiers can be used to prepare acetate transparencies for an overhead projector for presentations to larger audiences. Equipment is now available which enables information from a VDU or computer monitor to be projected by an overhead projector but as with colour photocopiers it is not common in small businesses. The same is true of computers with colour graphics display facilities and the ability to generate coloured acetates for overhead projector use.

This chapter therefore concentrates upon what is practicable for a small business. It describes what may be used not what must be used.

Tables

Tables have traditionally been used to present financial information. Accounts are a form of table. The advantages of tables are their precision and compactness. Unlike diagrams they do not have to be rounded off although this is sometimes done as a matter of choice.

There are some basic rules which improve many analytical tables.

There should preferably be not more than ten lines (rows) or columns with a break.

The break can be made by:

- A space.
- A change from lower case letters to capitals.
- Heavier ruling of say every fifth line.
- Short thicker (e.g. 5 mm) line on both edges of the paper and at the top and bottom maintains the readers' visual orientation.
- Light dry transfer shading or screening may emphasize a total or indicate a preference.
- Descriptions at the head of columns should not be written vertically because they cannot be read. They should be written diagonally. By using 5 × 5 mm square paper the diagonal lines can be drawn easily. If the columns need to

Exhibit 9.1 *Analysed sources of venture capital*

		Source A	Source B	Source C	Source D	Source E
Investments	Investor's contribution — Min. £K	6	25, 25	30, 30, 30	40, 45, 45	50, 50, 55, 55, 60, 90
	Investor's contribution — Max. £K	30	300, 600	400, 400, 1,000	600, 700, 800	600, 4,000, 1,000, 1,500, 2,000, 2,000
	Maximum contribution required from investee to match investor's minimum investment £K	7	19, 19	30, 24, 24	40, 30, 40	50, 45, 45, 50, 50, 50
Conditions and restrictions — Geographical	Midlands		×		×	×
	NE England			×	×	
	SE England			×		× ×
	SW England			×		
	NW England		×			×
	London			×	×	
	Scotland			×	×	
	Wales				×	×
Activity	Hi-tech	×			×	× ×
	Life science		×		×	×
	Medical			× ×	×	×
	Engineering					
Stage	Start-up	×	×	×	×	×
	Buy-out		×	×	×	×
	Buy-in		×	×		
	Rescue					
	Expansion			× ×	×	× ×
	Relocation				×	
	Rationalisation					×
	Pre-flotation					
Profits £K	50–100		×		×	×
	101–150			× ×	×	× × ×
	151–200					
	201–250					×

be wider, two spaces are used instead of only one as in the exhibit.

Exhibit 9.1 is an analysis of sources of venture capital for small businesses. It uses vertical spaces, heavier horizontal ruling, screening of the most attractive proposition (the first row) and diagonal segregated headings.

Diagrams

Diagrams do not communicate as much information as tables. Their advantage lies in the manner in which attention is attracted to the salient points if they are well prepared. As with tables it is possible to present a mass of detail which it is difficult to assimilate. The cardinal rule for diagrams of all types is therefore to have plenty of space in them.

The following diagrams are suitable aids to financial managements:

- *Graphs*. There are three types: line, profile and logarithmic.
- *Bar charts*. These are also known as column graphs. They may be vertical or horizontal.
- *Pie charts*.
- *Flow charts*. There are two types: block diagrams and networks, but horizontal bar charts are also used to show flow layouts of premises and plant.

Graphs

These are primarily drawn to show the relationship between two variables. *Time* is usually on the horizontal axis (the ordinate).

Exhibit 9.2 is drawn on 5 × 5 mm square paper not 'conventional' 2 − 10 − 20 mm graph paper in order to illustrate its advantages for giving the diagram space. Symbols are used to identify the four curves for different compound interest rates.

Words should not appear on the body of a graph. They should be at the side.

Exhibit 9.2 *Graph of continuously compounded interest charges/payments*
1   Curves drawn on 5 × 5 mm square paper then reduced. Symbols used to distinguish curves.
2   Dotted lines for October, November and December.
3   10% curve shows interest charged/paid monthly to be less than when continuously compounded.

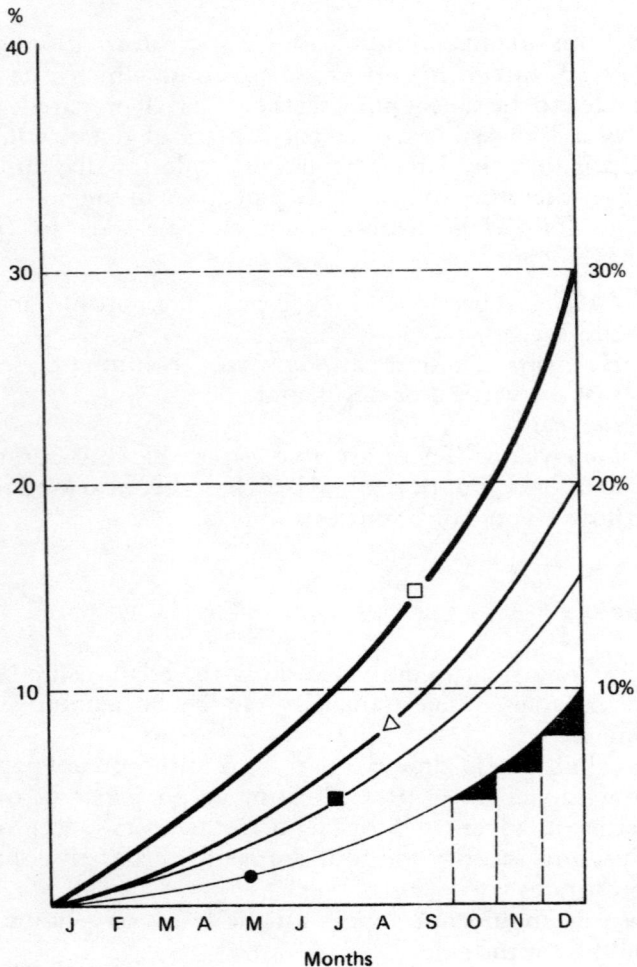

Months

Exhibit 9.3 *Profiles of income and expenditure*

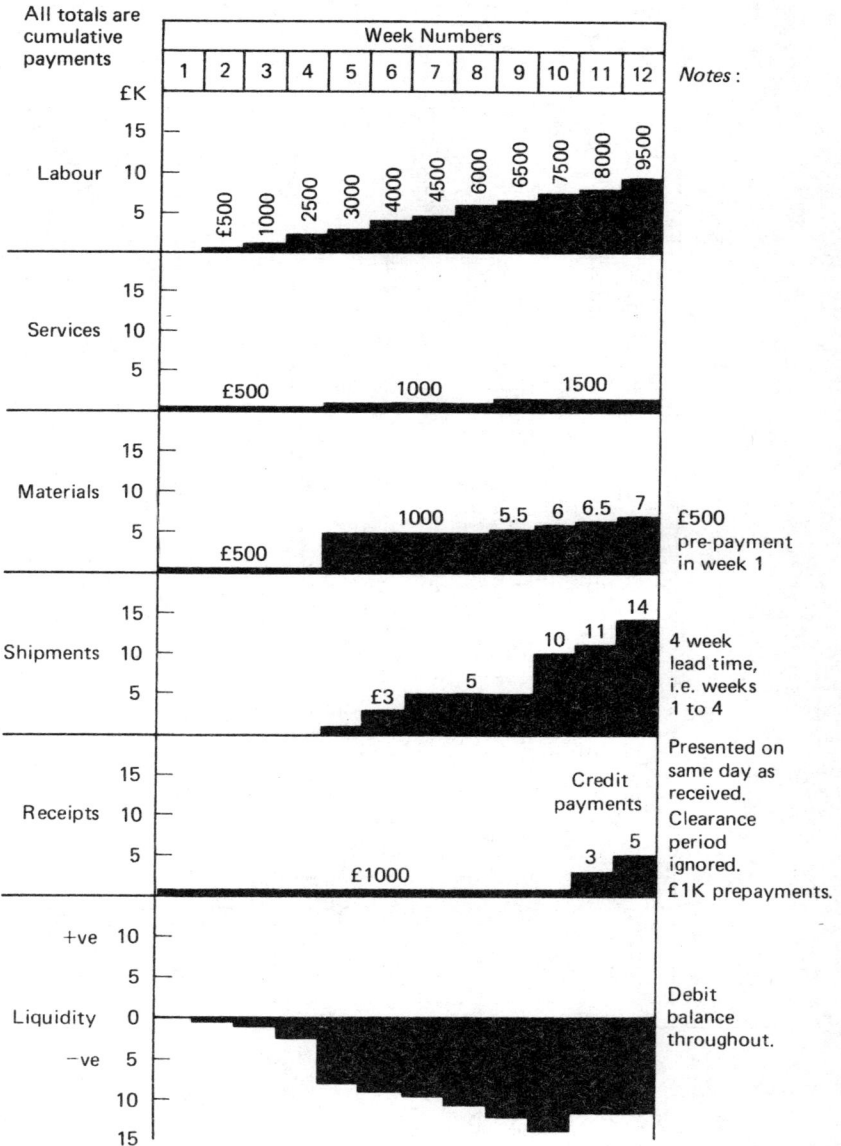

All totals are cumulative payments £K

Week Numbers 1 2 3 4 5 6 7 8 9 10 11 12

Labour 15 10 5

£500 1000 2500 3000 4000 4500 6000 6500 7500 8000 9500

Services 15 10 5

£500 1000 1500

Materials 15 10 5

£500 1000 5.5 6 6.5 7

£500 pre-payment in week 1

Shipments 15 10 5

£3 5 10 11 14

4 week lead time, i.e. weeks 1 to 4

Receipts 15 10 5

£1000 Credit payments 3 5

Presented on same day as received. Clearance period ignored. £1K prepayments.

Liquidity +ve 10 5 0 −ve 5 10 15

Debit balance throughout.

Notes:

Exhibit 9.4 *Cumulative sales turnover*
Note: Figures in brackets show gradually increasing increments although the line is straight. Reducing scale allows more data to be shown.

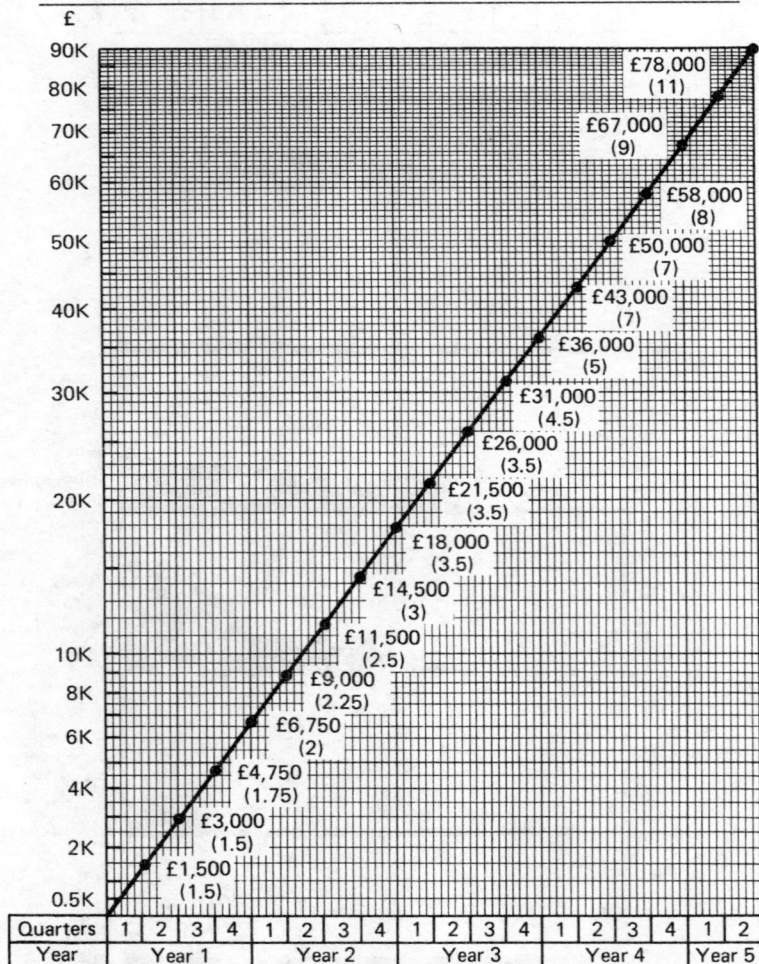

If pencil and pen lines are too indistinct and thicker felt pens produce lines with frayed edges when photocopied, flexible tape may be used. Exhibit 9.2 used a $\frac{1}{16}$ in and a ⅛ in tape. These flexible tapes are supplied with a dispenser.

Bar charts

Exhibit 9.3 uses conventional graph paper to produce profiles of income and expenditure for what could be a range of new products or some other situation similar to a start-up. If the grid lines are disconcerting they may be removed by lightening the photocopier image intensity. Alternatively squared paper may be used with a transparent overlay (e.g. acetate) if the lines are needed only to help with the construction of the graph.

Logarithmic graphs should not have their grid lines removed because the vertical scale gradually reduces. The horizontal scale is constant. This paper is occasionally used to compress the data associated with an extended time period.

Exhibit 9.4 shows the planned expenditure over such an extended period. It would not be possible to plot all this data on constant scale graph paper without minimizing the scale so much that its value as a visual aid would be seriously reduced. Single cycle log paper is used. Other log papers are primarily for scientific use and not suitable for illustrating financial information.

Exhibit 9.5 *Vertical segregated column graph.*
Note: The use of seven shades to segregate products after 50% reduction by photocopier.

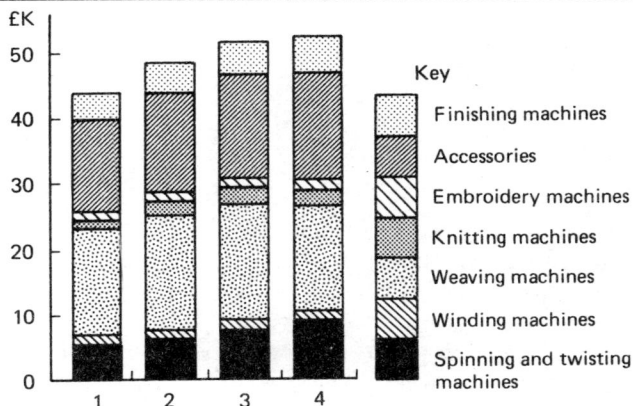

If a computer is unavailable, bar charts may be prepared on graph or squared paper for their preparation. The columns may be horizontal or vertical and represent positive and

---

Exhibit 9.6 *Suitable black and white shadings. Total of 36 choices.*

London (Round dots)	NE England (Diagonal lines)	SE England (Horizontal lines)	SW England (Square pattern)	NW England (Diamond pattern)	Midlands (Diagonal lines)	Wales and Scotland (Square dots)

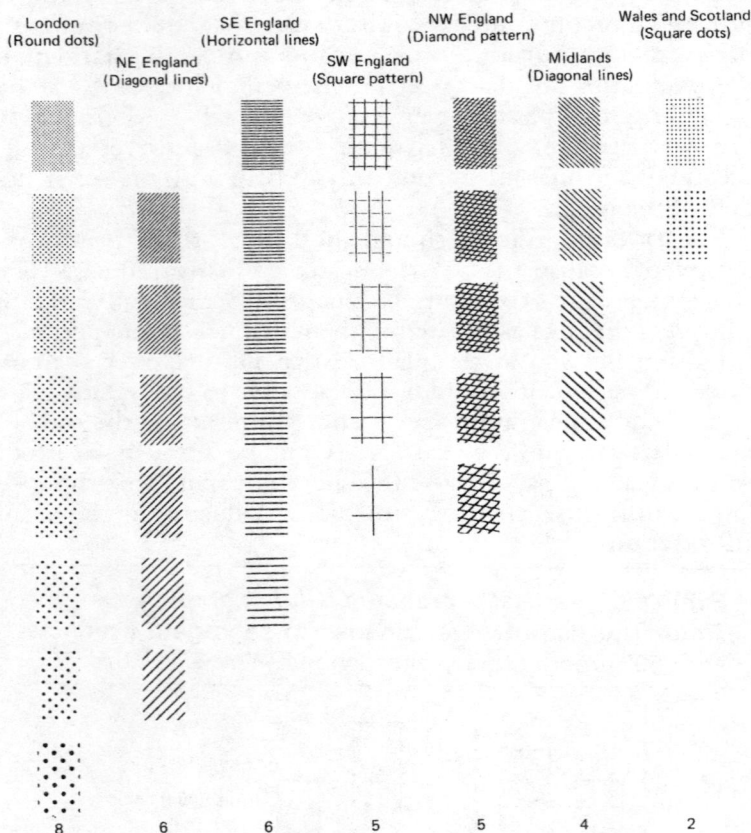

| 8 | 6 | 6 | 5 | 5 | 4 | 2 |

negative values (e.g. assets and liabilities, payments and receipts) against time periods. Columns can be placed alongside one another for comparison.

Exhibit 9.5 shows vertical columns which have been subdivided by shading to represent different amounts of income from different product groups. Although there are some thirty-six suitable types of shading, their use should be restricted and a legend placed in the margin to avoid confusion. Exhibit 9.6 shows the different types of shading available in dry transfer form.

Exhibit 9.7 *Horizontal bar chart for new machines. Original drafted on 5 × 5 mm squared paper. Photocopied with reduced intensity to eliminate light blue guidelines. Horizontal lines added after second photocopy.*

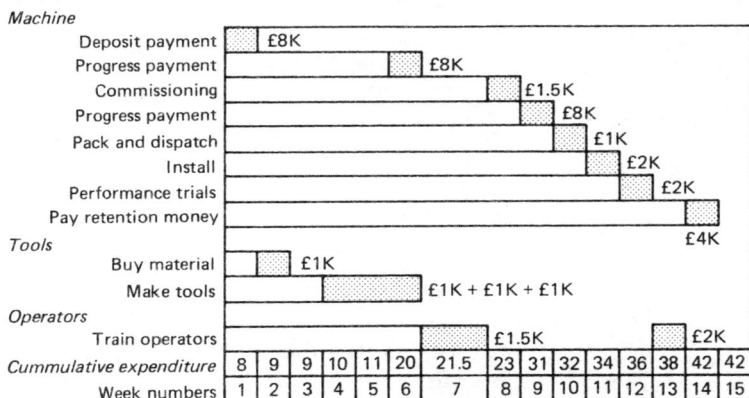

Exhibit 9.8 *Hybrid bar chart with negative and positive values and action cursor lines for cash flow.*
Shaded areas made from 55.10% adhesive backed translucent screen. Incremental lines were underneath the screen but visible. £20 k and lines drawn on the screen itself. Original drafted on 5 × 5 mm squared paper. Photocopying as Exhibit 9.7 to eliminate guidelines.

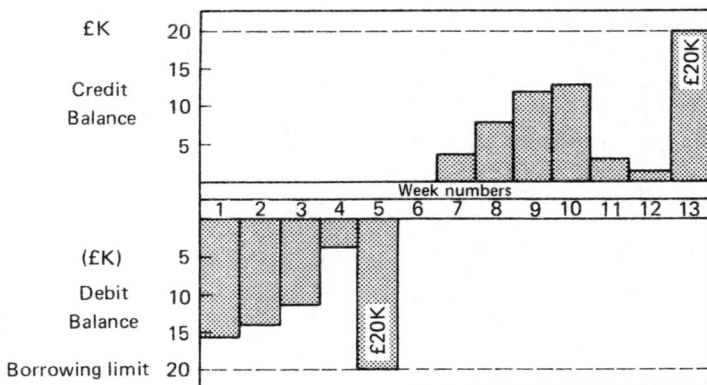

Horizontal bar charts are usually associated with illustrating the incidence of expenditure and duration of activities as in Exhibit 9.7. This was drawn on 5 × 5 mm square paper. It could have been drawn by a computer more quickly.

Exhibit 9.8 is a hybrid vertical bar chart on which action cursors are superimposed to indicate when action should be taken. With the increasing availability of software for financial management, computer graphics and video printers, this type of presentation may be preferred to the profiles illustrated in Exhibit 9.3. These however show the inter-relationships more clearly than Exhibit 9.8.

Pie charts

Unlike all the other diagrams described so far pie charts cannot be added to once they are drawn. They show 'how the cake is cut'. The data, money or percentages have to be converted into degrees. The equations are shown on Exhibit 9.9. The outer circle of degrees is only on the exhibit to show how easily they may be constructed. Normally they would not be shown. With the aid of a computer a pie chart can be prepared in about five minutes. Programs are available which enable the size of the chart to be selected, values given to each segment (wedge), labels appended and colour added.

3D effects are sometimes used to add prestige to diagrams, e.g. when they are being submitted to external financiers. Adding a 3D effect to a pie chart requires a graphic artist's set of French curves to join up the ends of the wedges or a computer with suitable software. Preparing Exhibit 9.9(b) required cutting and pasting as well, so the time spent in preparation may not be justifiable in a small business. Giving a 3D effect to straight lines is easy when one has isometric 3D paper as shown in Exhibit 9.10.

Flow charts

There are two types of flow charts. Their principal use is to promote thorough investigation by showing the inter-

Exhibit 9.9 *2D and 3D pie charts of costs*

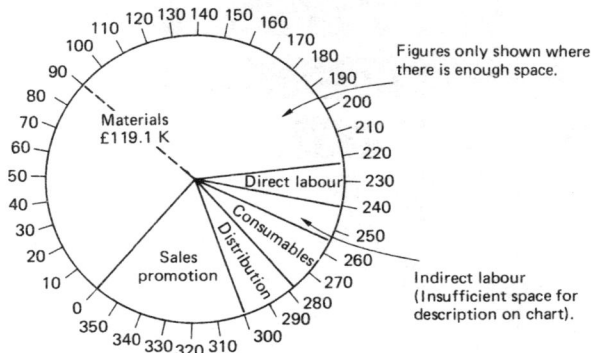

Degrees on protractor scale.
(Shown only for guidance to
explain construction. They
are not usually shown).

Figures only shown where
there is enough space.

Materials
£119.1 K

Direct labour

Consumables

Distribution

Sales
promotion

Indirect labour
(Insufficient space for
description on chart).

(a) Format

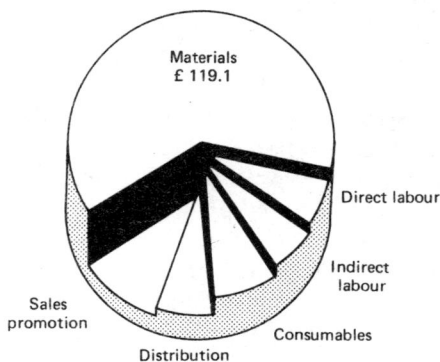

Materials
£ 119.1

Direct labour

Indirect
labour

Sales
promotion

Consumables

Distribution

(b) format

Expense item	Value £K	Percentage %	Degrees °
Materials	119.1	69	249
Direct labour	7	4	15
Indirect labour	6	3	13
Consumables	11	6	23
Distribution	10.	6	23
Sales promotion	19	11	40
Totals	172.10	99*	361*

*Error due to rounding up or down.

Exhibit 9.10 *3D horizontal bar chart*

Purchase analysis

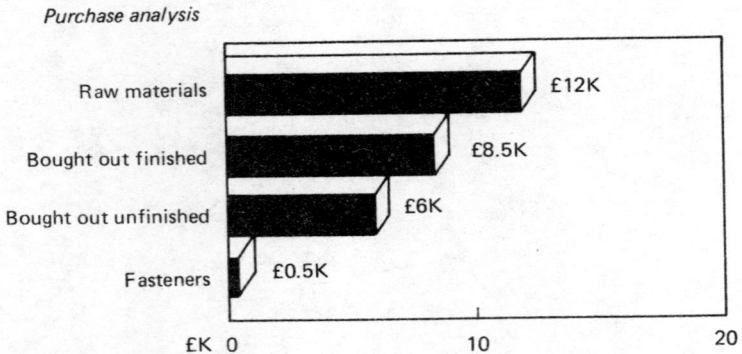

dependence of all the different relationships when a major exercise is undertaken.

Block diagrams cannot show so many activities (as will be seen from Exhibit 9.11) but a substantial amount of information can be written in the boxes. *Networks* show many more activities but in less detail. They originated as a tool for planning the manufacture of large civil engineering projects. They impose a strict discipline on the logical thinking processes of the person preparing them.

The reader may disagree with some of the logic in Exhibit 9.12. There are Pert computer programs which can process the times values allocated to each activity and show the critical path. Some programs have the additional ability to allocate resources (money) to the activities but this is best done manually. Different programs processing identical data can produce differing results.

The example in Exhibit 9.12 was not intended for computer processing. It is a combination of a network and algorithm showing both logical progressions and alternative routes.

Conclusion

This chapter has provided a range of alternative methods for presenting and illustrating financial data. Selective use of them will assist the manager in the task of overcoming the communication gap which constitutes a problem from time to time in many small businesses.

Exhibit 9.11 *Outline block diagram for business diversification*

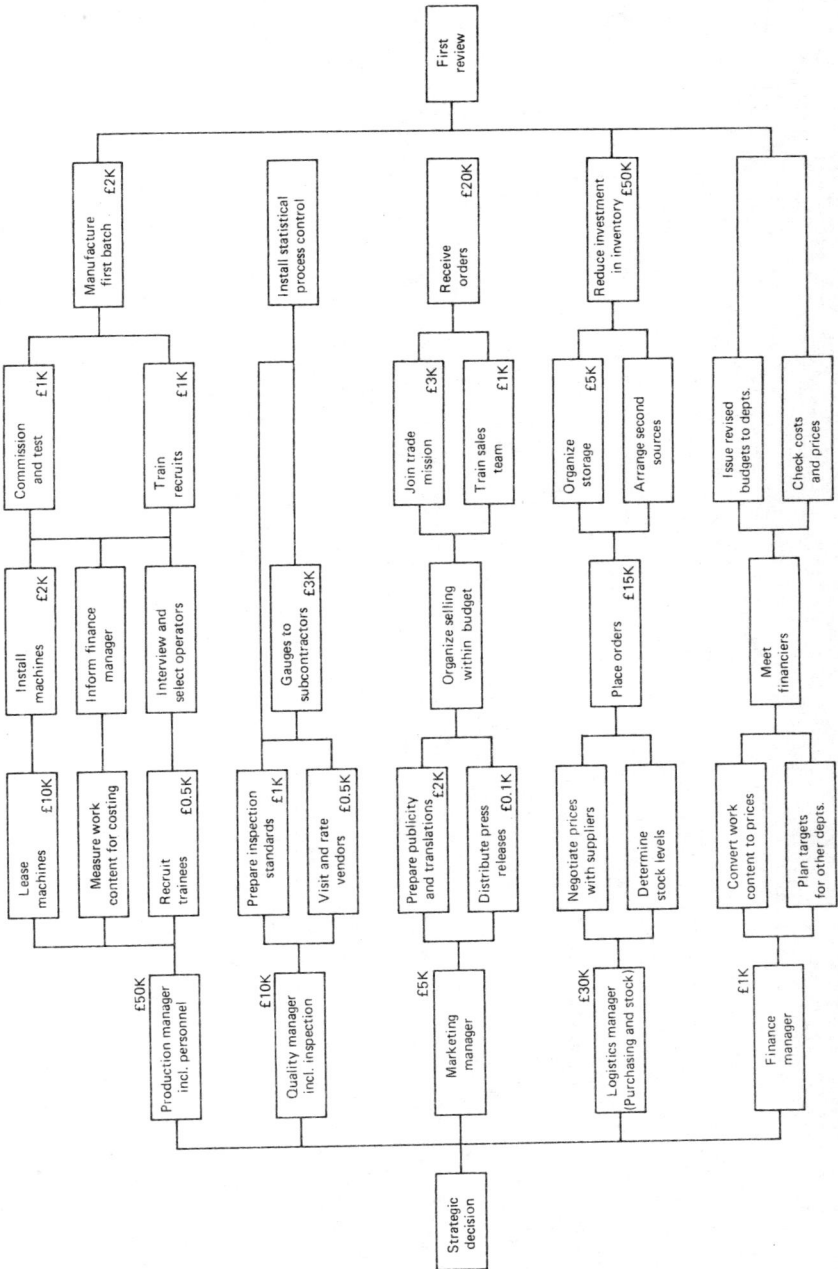

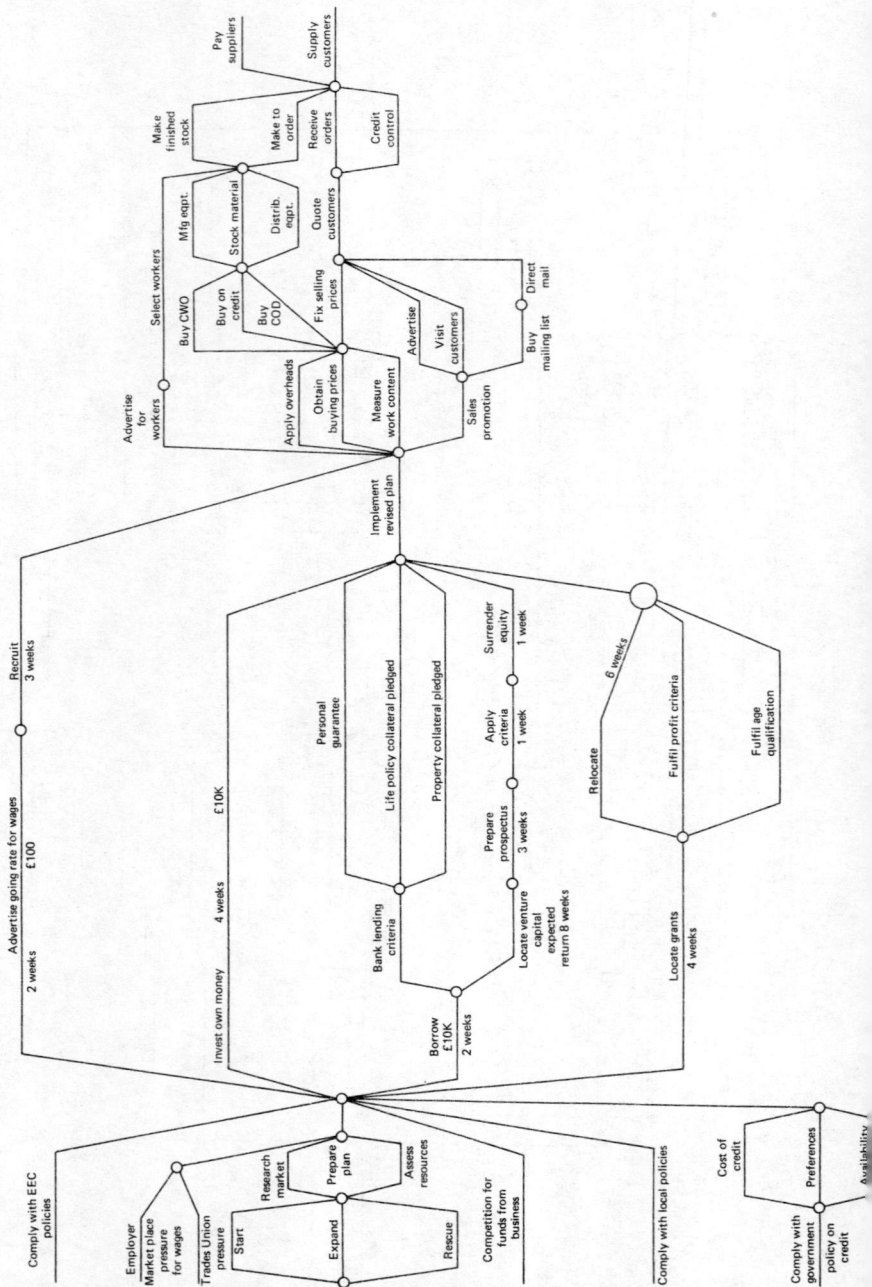

Exhibit 9.12 Hybrid network and algorithm chart for business start-up

Part Three   Specific Management Tasks

There is a range of specific tasks which call for the application of management skills other than systems and techniques.

10   Financial planning

Financial planning is a generic term embracing the different types of plan shown in Exhibit 10.1 alongside their scope and uses. It is also known as 'business planning'.

Composite plans

These are often the most difficult to prepare. Usually it is only these composite plans and dedicated plans which are seen by personnel outside the business.

The preparation of plans to be seen by personnel outside the business may be mandatory in so far as the majority of financiers demand them. At other times the manager may choose whether or not to prepare them.

Although some of their more specific uses are summarized in Exhibit 10.1 it is helpful to be aware of their associated *overall purposes*. There are three key words – accommodate, induce and match.

The financial effect of changes in circumstances have to be *accommodated*. These changes may be attributable to the gradual onset of a recession or boom. On the other hand, there is the sudden impact of a large order being received or unfortunately cancelled as sometimes happens. There may be an unexpected opportunity to acquire a building, a quantity of material or substantial facility at an attractive price.

Composite plans may serve the purpose of *inducing* changes, e.g. expansion. In this context the specific use of supporting an application for external finance has received considerable attention. Less attention has been given to their subsequent use for implementing changes once finance has been arranged and to their value for the regulation of the business as it develops.

Undergirding both the accommodation and induction of

changes, composite plans serve the purpose of providing a framework or decision support system for *matching* expectations from the business, actual and anticipated, with the resources, external and internal, available to it.

The difficulties of preparing composite plans can be formidable. Where they have the choice, some businesses respond to the difficulties by choosing not to prepare them.

There are difficulties in collecting meaningful quantifiable information on future events, opportunities, obstacles, restrictions and resources. As they form the basis of composite plans, *constituent plans* are subject to identical difficulties. Exhibit 10.2 lists the fortuitous factors and suggests the areas of financial management most affected by them.

The uncertainty attaching to the data permeates the relationship between the different items. If a profit margin or selling price is altered, the relationship between price and cost may change. Similarly, product mixes change and all products do not have identical profit margins. As mathematical techniques such as linear programming have yet to gain acceptance for small business financial planning, the manager is compelled to make assumptions which may be subjective.

Yet another difficulty is the importance which attaches to the composite plan by people and institutions external to the business. If a business is in need of external financial assistance, the acceptance of the plan can mean the difference between starting and not starting a business, between survival and liquidation or between expansion and stagnation. The person preparing plans in these circumstances must be aware that the recipients of the plan hold the destiny of the business in their hands and their prevailing attitude will be profit-motivated and not benevolent.

Businesses which have the money available to pay the fees of such advisers as accountants may therefore enlist their support – but that does not guarantee a favourable response by the recipient financier. Advisers and managers share a common difficulty when preparing plans. They are not sure what form and content the intended recipient of the plan expects it to take. As it may be necessary to approach more than one financier, the resulting plan may satisfy one person while another rejects it. Even writers of articles on financial and business planning are unable to agree on their format and content.

In view of this uncertainty the sections of this chapter which deal with these aspects of financial planning should be regarded as options and not stipulations.

Dedicated plans

Pensions and investments plans are described as dedicated plans and differ in many ways from composite or business plans. There is no shortage of specialists who offer their services in preparing them. Such specialists do not charge fees. They are paid on a commission basis – so it is in their interests to sell their services and products.

Action plans

Unlike dedicated plans, action plans are prepared on an ad hoc basis within the business often by departmental managers. The advantages derived from the implementation of action plans have to be seen to exceed the costs incurred in realizing those benefits. Not infrequently action plans have to satisfy certain criteria on profit margins and payback periods. They are most commonly but not exclusively associated with cost reduction exercises and may in the first instance owe their origin to a suggestion scheme.

Contingency plans

On the other hand, contingency plans may never be implemented because the circumstances which would necessitate their implementation never materialize. The need for contingency plans, of both kinds, is most appreciated when no such plans exist. Recourse has to be made to 'instant management' with its attendant risks and the danger of premium costs because likely situations have not been thought through in advance.

These financial plans are not the same as *budgets* although there are similarities. Budgets are prepared for shorter periods such as a year. They are usually subdivided into departmental

Exhibit 10.1 *Types of financial plans and their uses*

Category	Scope	Uses
Composite, consolidated or business plan	All financial aspects of the business and those aspects with financial implications	Immediate: Start up Survival and rescue Expansion Contraction Pricing Attraction of external support Eventual: Retention of external support Monitoring and control
Constituent plans	Profit Wages and salaries	Profit maximization in general Maximization of profit per £ of wages Avoidance of excess labour costs Acquisition and retention of an 'invisible' asset
	Inventory	Enhancement of return on capital employed Reduction in lead time and therefore servicing of work in progress Avoidance of interest charges

Category	Plan items	Objectives
Cash flow	Training; Research and development (products and markets); Sales promotion	Maintenance of liquidity; Continuity of supplies; Avoidance of interest charges; Credit management; Payment of taxes; Acquisition of an 'invisible' asset; Business growth; Increased turnover
Dedicated plans	Investment; Tax avoidance; Pensions and retirement	Maximization of income for business or an individual
Action plans	Cost reduction; Capital project appraisal; Recruitment; Market penetration	Reduction in unit costs; Increased profits and turnover; Improved asset utilization; Increased turnover and profits
Contingency plans	Windfall opportunity response; Cash reserves; Short-term borrowing; Subcontracting; Contract labour; Adversity response; Cash reserves (as above); Redundancy; Alternative facility financing; Reduction in capital employed; Disposal of assets	Maximization of short term income and profit; Extending market base and accumulating goodwill; Survival; Preservation of liquidity; Return to significant profitability

and sectional budgets whereas financial plans cover the whole business, cross departmental boundaries and relate to longer periods of time. The information contained in financial plans is therefore more rounded.

'Budget' in addition to the meanings used in this book has other meanings applied to it. Sometimes it signifies a ceiling or limitation on expenditure. Reference is made to having 'spent one's budget for the year'. At other times it is used to denote a target (e.g., for sales turnover). In this context the word 'target' is more specific. Its use implies aiming to reach a precise point, be it for sales turnover, stock turnover, wages awards, profits and/or the income from new customer accounts. There are also target dates laid down in connection with capital expenditure projects.

Besides being interchanged with 'budget' the word 'target' is often used to signify an 'objective'. However an objective is less precise than a target. In fact many targets may have to be achieved in pursuit of objectives similar to those cited on page 9. 'Improving service from stock to an unspecified extent' or 'reducing the manufacturing costs to the best of one's ability' or 'increasing market share' are examples of objectives. Management by objectives schemes involving individual managers also have financial implications.

The format and preparation of financial plans

The amalgamation of a complex array of targets, objectives, budgets, forecasts, resources, opportunities and financial figures into a coherent workable strategy is the essence of making composite or business plans. This section of the book concentrates on these because they are both difficult to produce and attract most attention outside the business. Sometimes they are as lengthy as prospectuses.

As these composite or business plans are increasingly required from small businesses by financiers to support applications for financial support, Exhibit 10.3 assumes that the end result is intended to be used in this way. Responsibility for the preparation of these plans rests with the manager. Even if professional advisers are retained there has still to be a large input by the manager.

By way of contrast, the preparation of dedicated plans (e.g. for investment) can be handed over to a specialist who will obtain quotations and submit them to the manager together with advice on which is the most suitable. Similarly action plans and the constituent plans which are eventually incorporated into composite plans can be prepared on behalf of the manager by someone else in the firm. Amendments can be made easily and oral explanations given when clarification is needed.

Single sheet composite business plans are sometimes preferred by financiers who do not wish to have a full format one. These are much simpler to produce, but they nevertheless have to be clear and relevant to the application being submitted even if they are brief. The manager is faced with having to decide what to include.

Exhibit 10.3 which is primarily intended for *full format* use will guide the manager on what to include or exclude, in a short form composite plan for the business. The aim in producing such a plan must be clarity and easy comprehension whilst emphasizing salient points.

There are two parts to the suggested layout. First there is a description of the business anatomy or architecture which is either directly of a financial nature or has financial implications. Second, there are financial statements which will differ with the stage of development which the business has reached. A new business cannot provide historical accounts nor can projections enter into the same level of detail as their historical counterparts.

The style is that used for report writing. Diagrams may be used to illustrate the financial statements (see Chapter 9). Reference data which interrupt the flow of the commentary on the business anatomy or architecture is best included in appendices (CVs for example, of key personnel and descriptions of fixed assets) if there are many items.

In addition to the factors mentioned at the beginning of this section, there are three other groups of factors without which meaningful composite or business plans cannot be prepared.

1 Decisions
2 Assumptions
3 Intervals

Exhibit 10.2 *Fortuitous factors with financial effects*

Category	Factor	Magnitude	Effects
Climatic	Rainfall	Above expectations	*Short term*
		Below expectations	Sales turnover
	Temperature	Above expectations	Cost of labour and materials from local and international sources
		Below expectations	Liquidity
			Stock turnover
Commercial	Competition	Increased	Overtime requirement
		Decreased	
Economic	Demand	Increase	*Longer term*
		Decrease	Profit margins
			Product and market diversification costs
	Supply	Increase	Research and development expenditure
		Decrease	Sales promotion expenditure
			Postponement or advancement of capital projects
	Inflation	Up	Business expansion or contraction
		Down	Recruitment or redundancy

Financial	Rates of exchange	Favourable Unfavourable	The effect of a factor on a business depends on whether the change constitutes an unforeseen obstacle or presents an unexpected opportunity
	Interest rates	Up Down	Some of the effects may be directly attributable to one factor
	Availability of credit	Up Down	A number of the effects are the result of more than one cause or factor
Fiscal	Taxation	Increase Decrease	Some short-term effects persist into the longer term
	Excise duties	Increase Decrease	

Decisions have to be made as to which are 'pacemaker' items. For example, are they fast response to sales orders or long production runs with longer sales lead times, short term gains or long term growth, diversification of market and products or concentration on fewer products and markets and lastly what margin to allow for fortuitous factors (see Exhibit 10.2)?

Assumptions have to be made on the relationship between different items and trends during the life of the plan. Market pressures on supply and demand are likely to change the relationship between selling prices, costs and profits. The relativity between labour and material costs can be disturbed by fluctuations at different times of different magnitude.

The assumption made regarding trends may have a political dimension. They have to take into account trends in inflation, interest rates, and exchange rates. The manager can assume that the trend is up, down or has levelled off. Not only are assumptions made on the direction of the trend but also the duration. Distinguishing between a 'blip' and a 'trend' is a related problem.

Information on the *intervals* between typical events in the life of the business is needed to determine how much time elapses before expenditure incurred generates income. Exhibit 10.4 lists some of the most significant time intervals which affect liquidity, cash flow and the achievement of profitability.

Exhibit 10.3 *Financial plan headings*

Part 1
1 Principal business objectives
    1.1 Short term (up to one year)
    1.2 Medium term (from one to five years)
    1.3 Long term (more than five years)
2 Products and/or services
    2.1 Range
    2.2 Advantages
    2.3 Outlets
3 Personnel
    3.1 Numbers and categories
    3.2 Key personnel (CVs may be included in appendices)
        3.2.1 Experience
        3.2.2 Qualifications
    3.3 Shortages
    3.4 Training programmes

4 Premises
  4.1 Layout (sketch may assist the description)
  4.2 Level of utilization
  4.3 General condition
5 Plant and equipment
  5.1 Numbers and categories (these may be listed in the appendices or taken from the fixed assets register)
  5.2 Level of utilization
  5.3 General condition
6 Customer base
  6.1 Domestic
  6.2 Export
7 Areas of risk and uncertainty
  7.1 Financial
  7.2 Sales
    7.2.1 Spread of customer base
    7.2.2 Spread of product base
  7.3 Logistics
    7.3.1 Supplies
    7.3.2 Distribution
  7.4 Vulnerability from competitors
    7.4.1 Commercially
    7.4.2 Technically
  7.5 Labour
    7.5.1 Availability
    7.5.2 Upward pressure on wages
    7.5.3 Industrial relations
8 Opportunities for growth
  8.1 Product improvement
    8.1.1 Design
    8.1.2 Manufacturing methods
  8.2 Market penetration
    8.2.1 Domestic
    8.2.2 Export
  8.3 Cost reductions
    8.3.1 Initial expenditure required
    8.3.2 Payback period and evaluation method used
    8.3.3 Product or resource affected

9 Obstacles to growth
   9.1 Market size
   9.2 Financial resources
   9.3 Manufacturing capacity

Part 2 Financial statement for submission to a financier
10 Actual and/or projected accounts
   10.1 Balance sheet
   10.2 Profit and loss account
   10.3 Trading account
   10.4 Cash flow statement or forecast
11 Intended use of additional finance
   11.1 Premises
   11.2 Personnel
   11.3 Plant
   11.4 Development
      11.4.1 Products
      11.4.2 Markets
12 Amount required
   12.1 Justification or commentary on 10 above
13 Time(s) required
   13.1 Lump sum
   13.2 Drawn down facility
14 Type of facility
   14.1 Loan
   14.2 Overdraft
   14.3 Equity participation
15 Repayment proposals
   15.1 Calculations of commencement date
   15.2 Possibility of delays
   15.3 Possibility of early repayment without
      penalties
16 Security
   16.1 Assets
      16.1.1 Business
      16.1.2 Personal or management
   16.2 Guarantees
      16.2.1 Personal
      16.2.2 Third party

Exhibit 10.4 *Significant time intervals for composite or business planning*

	From	Elapsed time to
Before receipt of orders	Submission of quotation	Receipt of order
	Application for finance	Completion of arrangements
After receipt of orders	Receipt of order	Sale of goods or service
	Receipt of supplies	Payment to supplier
	Sales to customer	Payment by customer
Developments	Acquisition of machine	Reduction in costs
		Sale of new or improved product
	Change of method and expenditure	Reduction in costs
	Product launch	Sales

The validation of financial plans

The process of validation is really the final stage of preparation. It is however worthy of separate treatment because the manager has to be ready to apply the same criteria to the finished plan as other recipients will. At the domestic level within the business there is the need to ensure that spending departments have not inflated their requirements in anticipation of a cutback and that income generating ones have not deflated theirs so that they can gain merit by exceeding their targets.

When financiers receive the finished plan they *may* use business ratios to evaluate it. The availability of computing facilities has made this much quicker and easier. Business ratios may be the source of considerable contention but they are widely accepted.

They vary considerably from one sector of industry or commerce to another and do not distinguish between large and small business.

At the planning stage, or immediately after it, only banks and venture capitalists have the opportunity to evaluate the plan by using ratios. They may well use published ratios for businesses engaging in the same activity as comparators. Although there are norms there is considerable spread on either side of them in the ratios published after accounts for many different sizes of undertaking have been analysed on a historical basis.

Besides being of assistance for validating plans by using criteria which others may use, the ratios assist the manager by directing attention to weak points in the business before anyone else may be aware of them. Fore-warned assists with being fore-armed. This operates against two time scales. First there may be the immediate one of applying for financial support. Second, much further into the future, is the need to prepare for the reactions of interested parties who will analyse the filed accounts of companies.

Conclusion

In the final analysis it is the actual achievements which have spending power, not predictions contained in plans.

11 Credit management

Credit management needs a combination of systems and subtlety. It is an art as well as a science. Both lax credit management and over zealous credit management can have disastrous effects.

Lax credit management is often cited as the reason for business failure. Even if bad debts are avoided, interest has to be paid by the supplier when a customer does not pay within the required time. Some customers treat their suppliers as a source of interest free working capital. Suppliers, from whose viewpoint this chapter is written, cannot withdraw credit facilities if there is a danger of a competitor taking the business and supplying the offending customer on future occasions.

Over-zealous credit management can also be detrimental to a business. Sales can be depressed because customers resent having to send cash with order. Incessant chasing even when accounts are overdue can also cause resentment. Some customers may react by placing future orders with competitors – and this has to be avoided.

Credit management is divisible into three parts:

1 Customer investigation.
2 The prevention of abuse.
3 Collecting overdue accounts.

The following terms are discussed in this chapter. Fuller definitions are given in the Glossary.

Aged debtor analysis	Endorsement
Airway bill	Escrow
Avalize	Factoring
Back to back credit	Forfaiting
Bad debt	Forgery
Bailiff	Forward contract

Bill of exchange
Bill of lading
Blocked funds
Certificate of posting
Charges forward
Cheque
Cleared balance
Commission
Confirming house
Credit agency
Credit insurance
Credit payment
Credit rating
Credit sales
Credit score
Crossed cheque
Currency swap
Current ratio
Deposit (1)
Discount (2a)
Discount house
Distraint
Doubtful debt
Draft
Forward cover
Garnishee order

Guarantor
Incoterms
Insolvency
Interest rate swap
Irrevocable letter
Mail payment
Middle rate
Noting and protest
Pre-payment
Proforma invoice
Progress payment
Quick ratio
Recourse
Revocable credit
Romalpa clause
Secured creditor
Short bill
Sight draft
Spot
Spread
SWIFT
Tenor
Uncleared balance
Writ
Z Score

Customer investigation

When a new customer wishes to open an account for which
credit facilities are granted, customer investigation is
appropriate. There are several methods of investigation which
may be used:

1   If the customer is a company, the latest filed accounts can
    be obtained from Companies House either by going there
    yourself or paying an agent to do so. As ten months are
    allowed for filing the accounts after the end of the
    company's year, accounts do not always reflect the

current trading situation. Nevertheless some suppliers use filed accounts for the calculation of credit days taken and the quick ratio (see Glossary). The latter should be higher than 0.8 if there are to be no doubts about a new customer's ability to pay. However, many businesses have much lower ones and are still supplied on credit.

2 Taking up references is a less scientific approach. The customer has to provide details of the bank and two or even three trade referees. Banks as a matter of policy protect the confidences of their customers and are careful about how much information is divulged. Moreover banks may know a customer's balances but not its total liabilities and assets at any one time.

Referees whose names are provided by a customer can hardly be regarded as impartial. A written impartial reference is unlikely to be given even if the application for information specifically releases the referee from obligations so there is no danger of incrimination.

3 Some managers therefore resort to using the telephone to obtain trade references regarding suitable credit limits and the promptness with which customers pay their dues. Off the record comments can sometimes be obtained in this way. They are seen by some as being of more value than formal written statements.

4 Credit agencies, in return for the payment of a fee, provide information on creditworthiness. Information on judgements against a customer is included. Names of credit agencies are listed in *Yellow Pages* under the 'Debt collectors' heading. Besides carrying out checks on creditworthiness they collect debts. Some deduct their commissions before paying out money collected. Others raise a separate invoice for the commission.

Preventing abuse

As customer investigation is in some ways unsatisfactory, many managers forego it but take steps to prevent abuse especially when first orders are placed by a new customer.

1 Large orders may require a deposit at the time they are

Exhibit 11.1

Except as otherwise expressly stated, this credit is subject to Uniform Customs and Practice for Documentary Credits (1983 Revision) International Chamber of Commerce Publication No. 400

Exhibit	*Adapted from an actual*	Date
Cable	*irrevocable letter of credit*	LC No.
Address	Name and address of	*ORIGINAL*
	issuing bank branch	BY AIR MAIL

To: Name and
address
of
Supplier (Beneficiary)

Our principal: (i.e. Customer)
Name and address

Dear Sirs,

We have opened our IRREVOCABLE LETTER OF CREDIT in favour of your goodselves for account of our principals named above, for any sum or sums, not exceeding in all amount . . . name of currency . . . basis FOB/CIF/FDD . . . available by negotiation/acceptance (delete one) of your drafts drawn on our principals at Sight or other tenor e.g. 45 days without recourse to you and accompanied by the following:

1   Your signed invoices in e.g. sextuplicate addressed to drawees certifying merchandise to be of UK origin and quoting reference number (for import). Invoices issued for amounts in excess of the credit amount are not acceptable.

2   Full set of clean 'shipped on board' bills of lading to order, bank endorsed and marked freight prepaid/payable at destination notify principals. Short form bill of lading prohibited. Bills of lading must indicate the name and address of both the credit openers and ourselves as notify parties. Bills of lading showing any additional charges payable over and above the freight are not acceptable unless specifically permitted in this credit. *This may be deleted for air shipments.*

3   Certificate of UK origin in e.g. quadruplicate issued by the Chamber of Commerce covering shipment of: quantity and description of goods.

4 Clean air consignment notes (No. 3 original for skipper) marked freight payable at destination addressed to ourselves notify applicant dated . . . latest and bearing LC Number as above.

5 Packing list in e.g. quadruplicate.

6 Special instructions.

One set of non-negotiable documents of five copies each of signed invoice, signed certificate of origin, unsigned airway bill, packing list to be forwarded direct to credit openers and a certificate to that effect should accompany original documents.

Other terms and conditions as per attached annexure which forms an integral part of this LC
Delete alternatives

Instruction/conditions

1 Shipment from: Shipment to:

2 Part shipment: 3 Transhipment:
permitted/prohibited   permitted/prohibited

4 *Bills of lading must be dated not later than* (may be deleted for air shipment).

5 Presentation of documents for negotiation must be made within . . . days of shipment date.

6 Documents must be presented for negotiation not later than . . . to our correspondents named below who must send to us original documents by air mail and duplicates by next air mail and claim reimbursement as marked by debiting us.

7 All bank charges outside (name of country) are for the account of beneficiary/credit opener.

8 Draft must be marked 'Drawn under' (name of bank)   LC number

Our correspondent's   Your faithfully
Bank in UK   Issuing bank
Name and address   Signature

placed especially if a customized product is ordered. Customers may then make enquiries about the supplier's creditworthiness.

2   Credit facilities may be granted up to a tightly controlled limit. By respecting this limit a customer is able to build up a track record and avoid the stigma of cash with order. For overseas customers such open account facilities should be carefully monitored.

3   Sometimes cash on delivery can be used for the collection of small amounts sent by post when there is a little possibility of repeat business. This is often less unacceptable than demands for cash with order. It is also available in many countries overseas.

4   Where larger sums of money are involved, granting credit facilities would not be prudent. Cheques accompanying orders may be dishonoured. The supplier may therefore ask for a *draft* to be sent with an order. Drafts are used both for UK and foreign business. They have to be paid for before a bank issues them. (Travellers' cheques are a type of draft because they have to be paid for at the time of issue.)

5   For even larger sums the safest method is to ask for an *irrevocable letter of credit* (see Exhibit 11.1). This is issued by a bank and certain documents have to be submitted at the time of shipment to the corresponding bank in the UK before the money can be released. If there is doubt about the validity of an irrevocable letter of credit it may be confirmed by a UK bank.

6   Where there is a degree of trust between a supplier and overseas customer, *bills of exchange* and *promissory notes* may be used to obtain payment (see Exhibits 11.2 and 11.3). Both these negotiable instruments require a signature by the customer but facilities for protest exist should there be a refusal. Avalization (see Glossary) is sometimes used. Bills and notes above a certain value can be discounted and some of their face value released to a supplier before the money is collected by a bank (see page 138).

7   When there is a possibility of slow payment rather than non-payment some managers unobtrusively apply a small percentage loading to the selling price (e.g. 2 or 3% to cover the cost of the interest).

Exhibit 11.2 Specimen Bill of Exchange

Supplier's (drawer's) Letterhead

Date
Serial number (e.g. same as
sales invoice)

Exchange for
123456 Name of currency, e.g. Whatsits

Anything Bought Inc.
21 The Route
Somewhere
Overseas (i.e. the customer or drawee)

(a) Example of sight or demand draft
At sight please pay this sole bill of exchange to our order the sum of ONE, TWO, THREE, FOUR, FIVE, SIX whatsits only for value received.

(b) Example of 45 day draft.
At 45 days after this first of exchange please pay to our order the sum of ONE, TWO, THREE, FOUR, FIVE, SIX whatsits for value received.

For and on behalf of
Everything Supplied Ltd
001 The Mount
Anytown

Status (e.g. Director)

Notes on specimen
1 The drawer has to sign on the back as well as the front using the wording and layout as shown.
2 The word 'draft' is often used to denote a bill of exchange although it also has other meanings (See Glossary).
3 Bills of exchange which are drawn payable after a certain number of days have to be accepted (i.e. signed) by the buyer.
4 Special stationery is available from stationers but its use is not mandatory.

Exhibit 11.3

```
· PROMISSORY NOTE ·                      For  DM 5,500,00
                                                      Amount in figures
          SPECIMEN
   Anytown                              30 November 1065
          Place and Date of Issue                    Name of month in letters
          30 February 1066
On..............................................................against this promissory note I (We) promise to pay
To.....Nothing Lacking Suppliers GmbH.......................................................or Order

   the sum of:  Deutsche
                Mark              Fivethousandfivehundred
                                          Amount in words

   FOR VALUE RECEIVED
                  XYXX Bank      Sort Code 99  99  99      An Ideal Customer Ltd
   payable at:    21 The Summit  Account 099099           1001 The Valley
                  Sometown                                Anytown          John Smith
                                                          Signature and full address of maker
```

8   Adding a 'Romalpa' clause to a sales invoice to the effect
    that goods remain the property of the vendor until
    payment is received in full is a common practice, but it
    cannot be recommended as being a universal panacea for
    credit abuse. The problem is that of recovering goods in
    the event of non-payment by the customer. The goods
    may have been permanently assembled with other goods
    or sold to a third party.

Collecting overdue accounts

Overdue accounts are the accounts of customers to whom
credit facilities have been granted but who have not paid
within the required time. Some customers may object to the
credit terms because they conflict with the terms of purchase
on their orders. The manager has therefore to anticipate this
response by stating settlement and overdue surcharge terms
(e.g. 2% at the time of quoting, that is, before goods are
supplied). However, not all goods are subject to quotation so
settlement terms should appear in price lists. Customers may
try to countermand these with their conditions of purchase.

   Some businesses try to avoid the unpleasantness which can
be associated with collecting overdue accounts by offering a
large cash discount for early settlement, for example 5% for
payment within seven days.

   Despite these precautions there are still difficulties associated with collecting overdue accounts. A number of methods
are in use to overcome this problem.

1 The polite written reminder is often replaced by a polite telephone call as soon as an invoice becomes due for payment.

2 If there is no response a more firmly worded letter referring to the earlier reminder and requesting immediate payment follows. Recorded delivery must be used for the letter.

3 A stop may be placed on future supplies until the unpaid account is brought up to date.

4 Persistent offenders may have their credit facilities withdrawn.

5 Businesses which factor their invoices can transfer the collection of accounts to the factor in return for the payment of a service charge to cover the administration of the sales ledger. The onus for collection is then placed on the factor which takes some of the pressure away from personnel in a small business.

6 If litigation has to be used to recover a debt, the involvement of a solicitor is recommended. It is preferable to choose one with a computerized debt collection service. The County Court procedures, whilst being accessible to all businesses, present difficulties because they are unfamiliar to the manager who only occasionally uses their services.

If the sums of money owed by a company are large a solicitor will be needed to take the claim to the appropriate court.

Recovering debts from overseas customers can be very difficult so it is customary to have some form of indemnity insurance. Unless the initial contract states which legal system is to be used in the event of a dispute there can be lengthy legal arguments as to whether a foreign or English legal system applies. It may be necessary to employ lawyers in the UK who are familiar with the laws of the offending country. Their charges are high because they have special skills.

Pursuing actions through the courts necessitates certain proofs. These relate to evidence of dispatch and the absence of complaints about the goods, during a reasonable time, from the customer.

Conclusion

If it is not true to say of credit management that prevention is better than cure it is true to state that prevention is easier than cure.

12   Insurance

Insurance is an extensive and complicated subject. In the business world the word 'insurance' has both general and specific meanings. As it is a complicated subject this chapter does not claim to be an exhaustive treatment. Its aim is to state the manager's responsibilities and to give guidance on the common types of business insurance, its sources and its benefits. Many of the terms used by the specialist insurance industry appear in the Glossary. The following insurance terms are defined:

Act of God
Actuary
Agent
Airway Bill
All risks insurance
Assurance
Bill of lading
Bond (3)
Broker
Business interruption
Certificate of insurance
Certificate of posting
Commission
Cover (2)

Credit insurance
Directors' and officers' liability cover
Employer's liability insurance
Fire insurance
Insurance
Loss adjuster
Loss assessor
Marine insurance
Policy (2)
Public liability insurance
Reinsurance
Term insurance
Underwriter (2)

Before describing the specialist insurance with which this chapter is primarily concerned, general insurance must be mentioned. A well managed business makes its own arrangements independent of the insurance industry. There are two types of arrangement to make, general and special:

1   *Procedural insurance.* This is concerned with the installation and operation of procedures to reduce or, better still, to

eliminate the scope for fraud and dishonesty within the business. Internal auditing is an example of procedural insurance. Unlike insurance policies issued by insurers there is no stated content, starting and finishing date, exclusions, stipulations, and possible extensions.

2 *Buying forward.* This is another type of general insurance, in that it seeks to protect the business from the adverse effects of a deterioration in the international current exchange rate by buying forward to pay for imports. The wisdom of doing this is questioned by some managers because exchange rates can improve as well as deteriorate. Of course, this type of 'general insurance' is not relevant to all small businesses.

Parts of the specialist insurance industry are however relevant to all small businesses.

Sometimes insurance is compulsory but many types are discretionary.

The purpose of insurance

Insurance owes its existence to the fact that every business risks being harmed by the occurrence of adverse events and circumstances. The purpose of insurance is to neutralize their effects and place the business in the same position as it enjoyed prior to the loss being incurred. It is a safeguard, and the following examples show how this safeguard can work.

A policy taken out by a business on the life of a key executive is for the purpose of providing compensation to the business in the event of that executive's death. The compensation could be used in several different ways to alleviate the loss of that key executive's services.

Policies taken out to cover premises, plant, stock, work in progress, and turnover in connection with a business interruption policy or personnel, are likewise for safeguarding the business against primary and consequential losses. The reasons for the loss may be accidental or malicious. However if an executive of insured business, experiencing trading difficulties set fire to the premises, that would be a criminal act. Payment would be refused by the insurer. The purpose of insurance is not to cover trading losses.

The insurance industry

The service which the specialist insurance industry provides to a business is one which enables risks stated in insurance proposals and subsequently detailed in policies to be spread amongst businesses which share the same risks. By collecting a premium from all the businesses which are at risk, a fund is accumulated for paying out money to any businesses which suffer loss when the risk becomes a reality.

The premium paid reflects the probability of the risk becoming a reality, an estimate of its magnitude and the duration of the cover. The annual premium on a policy of three years' duration would be less than for a policy with one year's duration. High risks attract high premiums. There are some risks which insurers refuse to accept.

Within the insurance industry there are specialist branches associated with certain types of risk. Exhibit 12.1 lists the common ones.

There are also specialist personnel employed by different organizations. Independent brokers are the intermediaries between insurers and businesses. Inspectors employed by insurance companies are concerned with attracting new business from brokers and by direct approaches to businesses. The manager of a business may also have contact with surveyors and valuers. If a claim is made there may be contact with loss assessors and loss adjusters. Meeting actuaries and underwriters is less frequent in a small business.

One problem of dealing with the insurance industry is its use of legal language in its policies. Certain insurance companies however are now using plain English.

Common types of insurance

Some types of insurance are compulsory as defined by statute so care must be taken not to overlook them. In this category are:

- Employer's liability.
- Motor insurance.
- Plant inspection insurance.

Exhibit 12.1 *Common types of business insurance*

Category	Section	Content	Extensions	Restrictions and exclusions	Notes
Property	Fire and Perils	Loss or damage to buildings and/or contents by fire, lightning or explosion of domestic boilers.	Special perils: aircraft and aerial devices, explosion, riot, civil commotion and malicious damage, earthquake, storm, tempest, flood, bursting, overflowing water pipes and apparatus, impact by own road vehicle, third party road vehicle, horses, cattle, sprinkler leakage.	First £250 of damage	Additional amount should be included to cover architect's and surveyor's fees and debris removal. Target property (e.g. non-ferrous metals and video equipment) to be listed separately. Details of occupancy, construction and proximity to waterways and railways for proposal.

Theft	Entry to and exit from premises by forcible and violent means or robbery. Damage up to 20% of sum insured.		
	Loss or damage to buildings	First £250 of loss or damage Silvered, embossed, lettered, bent or ornamental (see next column).	Applies to: ornamental, engraved, lettered or painted, toughened, stained, enamelled, embossed, skylights, cut plate, lamps only if they are specified
Glass	Breakage, cost of boarding after breakage, damage to window frames.	First £50 of loss	
All risks (see Glossary)			

Business		Accidental damage to internal vending machines, typewriters, accounting machines, music relay and public address systems, telephones.
Engineering	Boiler and pressure plant, lifting gear, mechanical and electrical plant.	Inspection and fragmentation damage, temporary repair. Sudden and unforeseen damage.
Computers	Repair and replacement after breakdown not recoverable	

	under a maintenance agreement.		
Business interruption	Loss of net profit. Payment of continuing overheads, wages and salaries. Expenditure for keeping a business going. Professional fees.	Theft if not insured elsewhere. Denial of access to property due to damage by insured peril to neighbouring premises. Damage at sub contractors', customers', storage premises and sites.	A form of average applies so the sum insured must be adequate. Indemnity period should not normally be less than one year
Money	Loss by theft or accident. Personal accident and assault benefits.		In transit, in safe or strongroom, on premises.

Goods in transit	Own goods in own vehicles, loading and unloading risks. Consigned goods	Loss or damage in UK.	Specified vehicles. Road, rail, post. Exports and imports separately covered by one off or declaration marine policy
Liabilities	Employer's	Indemnity for legal liability for injury to employees.	Proposal requires details of types of labour and plant.
	Public	Indemnity for legal liability for injury to and damage to third parties occurring accidentally and arising out of the business.	Claimant's expenses included.

Product	Indemnity for legal liability for injury to and damage to third parties occurring accidentally and arising out of goods sold, supplied, erected, repaired, altered or installed.	Claimant's expenses included. Separate details required for USA.
Directors' and officers'	Indemnity against claims by shareholders for negligence.	Malpractice excluded.
Legal expenses	Pursuing and defending legal action for the business.	

			Obtainable from insurers, invoice factors and Export Credit Guarantee Department.
Book debts		Loss arising from an inability to collect debts after destruction of records.	
Fidelity guarantee		Loss due to fraud and/or dishonesty by employee(s)	
Indemnity	Credit	Indemnity against bad debts and late payments	
	Professional	Indemnity against claims for bad advice by consultants	

Life	With profits (endowment)	Payment of an insured sum plus profits in the event of death or survival to maturity of the policy.	
	Without profits	Payment of the sum insured at death or at maturity.	
	Term (key person)	Payment of the insured sum at death.	Used to cover life policies pledged as collateral for overdrafts and loans.

National Health Insurance is also compulsory and subject to an efficient collection procedure which prevents any employer overlooking it.

Providers of finance for assets, (for example, mortgaged buildings, hired and leased plant) may stipulate the amount of insurance cover to be taken out by the business. Some financiers even specify the insurer.

The second type of insurance is that where the business is free to decide whether or not to insure. Insurance is at its discretion. Insurance of property, glass, business equipment, computers, business interruption, money, goods in transit, legal expenses, book debts, fidelity guarantees and bonds together with private medical insurance and travel insurance are in this large category. (See Exhibit 12.1.)

Arranging cover

Arranging insurance cover is in many respects similar to buying any other service for a business. Potential suppliers have to be located and a draft specification prepared so that quotations can be obtained.

As with other services there are potential suppliers of a service who will ask to be excused from quoting. It is uneconomic for large brokers to deal with small businesses so they are unable to respond to their insurance needs. Brokers who operate from High Street shops may not offer all the types of insurance which a business needs. The manager may therefore have to use trade directories to locate a suitable insurer. Among the insurance brokers listed in *Yellow Pages* there is usually a small number who handle the insurance needs of small businesses.

Once a possible insurer has been located there may still be difficulty in arranging certain types of cover. For example insurers dislike duty deferment bonds. They may therefore insist on all the insurance needs of the business being placed with them before accepting the risk of an unattractive type of insurance such as a bond.

If a broker is being used and there is a choice of insurers, quotations from different insurers have to be compared. The principal items for comparison are:

1 The content of the insurance.
2 Any exclusions.
3 The possibility of extending cover. It may be possible to include items normally excluded by extending a policy.
4 Stipulations like required expenditure on security locks and sprinkler systems.
5 The premium to be paid.
6 Provision for inflation, e.g. by escalators of say 5 or 10% or Day 1 clauses on the value of property up to 50%

Ideally the promptness with which claims are settled should influence the choice of insurer, but that information is not always easy to obtain. Settlement of claims without delay is vital to many small businesses which cannot call up reserves to sustain their trading while claims are being processed.

Arranging some types of insurance cover is relatively easy because the insurance is conveniently packaged, clearly stated and attractively presented. Overseas travel insurance is an example. Travel agents and charge card companies act as brokers. These insurance packages are often cheaper and more comprehensive than those obtainable from commercial insurers who offer a wider range of services.

Insurance taken out immediately before the despatch of goods overseas is also easy to arrange. The invoice value of the goods, their destination, and the cost are known precisely. There is no necessity for estimates and forecasts which frequently cause problems for small businesses.

Private medical insurance is similarly available in a conveniently packaged form for both the UK and overseas. There are a number of packages on offer so there is no difficulty in obtaining cover should it be required. Care has to be taken if the insurance relates to long periods away from the UK. Expiry dates can pass unnoticed.

Before paying the premium some businesses may decide that it is neither economic nor beneficial to arrange cover. Those with adequate resources may consider it advantageous to accept the risk themselves rather than pay a specialist insurer to do it. The majority however choose to transfer the risk to a specialist organization. They are more skilled in calculating the probability and magnitude of risks than the personnel of a small business.

Obligations to insurers

Besides paying a premium, in return for the safeguards provided by insurers there are other obligations placed on businesses:

1 Businesses which are slow payers of premiums may be taken off cover. This is tantamount to being disowned by the insurers. Insurers are not to be regarded as an unofficial source of working capital.
2 Businesses should not expect to profit from any reimbursement resulting from a successful claim for compensation.
3 When submitting a claim, accurate descriptions of times and circumstances supported by sketches where appropriate are needed. A sketch often communicates more than a lengthy description. If the claim is contested by an insurer other than one's own the evidence may be challenged by lawyers acting on behalf of the opposing insurer. Legal proceedings may be involved.
4 Care has to be taken to protect whatever is insured lest any claim for reimbursement be invalidated. Precautions should be taken against exposing individuals to undue risks. Issuing instructions to cashiers on how to react when confronted by would-be thieves is one such precaution when the business has a money insurance policy. Combustible waste should be frequently cleared. Precautions should be taken against fire risks when welding and when applying cellulose paints.
5 The insurance cover should bear some resemblance to reality. Businesses which are under-insured could be penalized if a claim were made. On the other hand over-insurance would gain nothing as the purpose of insurance is to place the insured in the same position as it enjoyed before the loss was incurred.
6 All statements on proposals and claims should be honest. Proposal forms invariably require an undertaking to be signed regarding the accuracy of the statement in it.

13   External finance

After plans, even embryonic ones, prospectuses and brochures have been prepared, possibly as part of the financial planning process, there may not be sufficient money available within the business for it to embark on its planned course of action or to sustain a desirable level of activity. Additional money may need to be introduced from external sources, and there may be difficulty in finding a source of finance.

The majority of these sources of finance constitute a form of borrowing. It takes many different forms. There are loans from institutions and individuals, factoring and discounting of negotiable instruments, overdrafts and sales of shares in companies. The time during which these facilities is available to a business varies from the short term to several years.

Besides borrowing facilities, some businesses may qualify for grants which will have conditions attached to them.

Reasons for seeking external finance

The reasons for seeking external finance vary greatly. Some businesses are temporarily unable to exist without borrowing to pay wages and purchase supplies.

The circumstances which give rise to this situation are diverse. Businesses starting up have had no opportunity to generate income for ploughing back into the business. Those with large contracts need external finance so that they may be completed. Businesses emerging from a difficult trading situation need temporary assistance. Finance may be needed to acquire another business. Similarly external finance may be necessary when a business has an opportunity to increase sales but needs additional working capital to do it. The same is true of product and market development or the purchase of assets.

Businesses which have money available for all the above situations may nevertheless choose to borrow it in the full knowledge that it will be more expensive than using their own. This may appear unwise but there can be good reasons. First is the desire to survive a downturn without having to negotiate with lenders from a position of weakness. On the other hand it may also avoid the time consuming quest for external finance if there is a sudden upturn in the order book. The second reason is the policy of some businesses towards spreading the risk and having a broad financial base. It has been said 'It is better to risk someone else's money than one's own'.

Reducing the need for external finance

As the cost of external finance is usually high, especially for small businesses, the majority try to reduce the need for it. Only grants and some soft loans are available at less than prevailing market rates. Reducing the need however is not the same as under-estimating requirements. It is better to be able to justify the optimum sum required, but be offered less, than to start from a lower threshold and have that reduced to a figure which is unworkable.

Renting, hire purchase, mortgaging and remortgaging, sale and leaseback are frequently used to acquire assets. In these ways lump sum payments are avoided. While repayments are quarterly or monthly liquidity is preserved and the need to seek additional finance avoided. The disadvantage is that in the long term the cost is higher than outright purchase because financiers, except in special cases, charge market rates of interest.

In the short term the cost of labour may be reduced by sub-contract and outwork or by employing temporary labour from an agency. This eases the need for space, premises and sometimes equipment as well. Long term commitments associated with recruiting permanent labour for an uncertain market are avoided although there is a premium cost to be paid.

Suppliers who offer credit facilities also reduce the need for finance. New suppliers often require cash with order. Unless asked for credit terms on subsequent occasions, suppliers will continue to ask for cash with order irrespective of the delivery lead time for the goods or service. Managers should take care not to abuse credit terms lest they be withdrawn.

Charge and credit card companies advertise the delayed payment facilities which use of their cards bring to businesses both for UK and overseas expenses. Travellers' cheques and foreign currency do not have to be bought and paid for in advance if such cards are used. Credit cards attract high rates of interest, they can be stolen and used too liberally. Nevertheless they do make a contribution to reducing the need for external finance even if they themselves are a form of such finance.

Sources of external finance

There are several sources of finance. It should not however be assumed that finding one which is prepared to support a business will be easy. The following are possible sources:

1 *Local, national and European governmental agencies.* Grants and loans are made on preferential terms by local and national government departments and by the European Economic Commission. The primary aim is to benefit the community as a whole. Small businesses in certain geographical areas or industries are eligible to apply for some of the money.

   There are two methods of administration. The money may be made available at the outset, but often the money has first to be spent and then reclaimed. The business has therefore to have sufficient money in the first place. Moreover the grant or loan may not be for the full amount of the expenditure to which it relates.

2 *Trusts.* Charitable trusts sometimes make small amounts of money available to specific groups of people starting a business (for example, the Prince of Wales Youth Trust).

   Trusts cannot be regarded as a major source of business finance.

3 *Suppliers.* Suppliers of capital equipment make arrangements for leasing, renting and hire purchase. The collateral resides in the asset. Before the facility is made available the

supplier has to be assured that the required payments can and will be made otherwise the goods may be recovered.

Credit facilities granted by suppliers of goods used regularly by the business should be not regarded as a source of working capital.

4   *Customers.* For large contracts customers may be willing to make payments on deposit and subsequent progress payments as specified stages of the contract are completed. Before doing this the customer needs to be assured that the business will not fail, for in the event of the business failing, the customer would lose the deposit and never receive any goods.

5   *The business itself.* Provided a business is already trading and raising sales invoices, it may be possible to factor or discount invoices, bills of exchange and promissory notes. Factors and invoice discounting companies will 'buy' sales invoices and make advances immediately to the business up to an agreed limit of their value (for example 79%). Interest at a higher than market rate will be charged on the advance. These companies need to be assured that the debts are sound and unlikely to go bad when they try to collect the money due against the invoice.

There are variations on the arrangement which enable businesses to retain control of their sales ledger as in invoice discounting. The customer is not therefore aware that an outside financier is involved with the business. Margins have to be sufficient to cover the charges. Some businesses have prospered by using this method of financing.

The discounting of bills of exchange and promissory notes is not such a ready source of finance. Banks and acceptance houses impose minimum amounts below which it is uneconomic for them to accept these negotiable instruments (this may, for example, be £30,000).

6   *Banks. Clearing banks* offer, but do not always agree, to lend through overdrafts and loans. They are often the first point of contact because they are easily approached as there are numerous branches. If one bank refuses to grant a facility a nearby one can be approached. Unsecured loans, if they are available, are for small amounts at surcharged rates of interest. Their use for business purposes may even be forbidden.

A business therefore has to be prepared to secure the facility by collateral, personal guarantee or a fixed and floating charge on the assets of the business if it is already trading. Rates of interest charged are often higher for small businesses.

Secondary banks which offer loans to householders through their press advertising are not a recognized source of business finance.

Merchant banks finance large projects. The small business may have contact in connection with counter trade or large projects to which it is a contributor. If merchant banks are to become involved with management buyouts and buy-ins for the larger small companies, the initial contact is usually through one of the large accounting firms who specialize in this branch of finance.

7 *Venture capital.* Provided by both institutions and individuals. Venture capitalists, in return for taking high risks, require a stake in the equity so the business has to be incorporated. The venture capitalist's ultimate aim is to achieve a return better than market rates either by regular income or by the sale or shares to make a capital gain. Responsibility for running the business rests with the management but there may be nominee directors appointed to the board by the venture capitalist. The business invariably has to be trading and there are minimum amounts of money below which venture capitalists are not prepared to consider becoming involved. (See Exhibit 9.1.)

Difficulties

In the previous section on *Sources of external finance* a number of difficulties were mentioned. There are yet more . . .

1 *Locating sources of finance.* With the exception of clearing banks who advertise their services in the media and have a prominent presence in the High Street, many other potential sources of finance have an almost invisible profile. The financial press carries a small number of advertisements from institutions and individuals. A number of them appear under box numbers so the

identity of the advertiser is hidden. The manager may therefore deem it unwise to reply lest the information be channelled to a competitor.

2 *Requirement of a track record.* All financiers, institutions and individuals require a track record from the applicant for financial assistance. Cynics say that financiers are more interested in where you have been than in where you are going. The track record of the principal is important for the smallest of small businesses. Their larger counterparts are expected to show a profitable growth.

3 *Debt servicing.* Financiers expect that applicants with an acceptable track record will be able to service the debt by repaying interest and principal at the stated times.

4 *Small business failure rates.* Financiers are fearful, especially when businesses are starting, that they will not survive. There is therefore a danger that any money advanced may be irretrievably lost. The failure rate may be as high as 50% of all start-ups in certain small business sectors. The manager trying to negotiate a facility has therefore to overcome a formidable credibility hurdle.

5 *Minimum and maximum limits.* Venture capitalists, factors and invoice discounting companies impose minimum limits below which they are not interested in applications for finance. Factors and invoice discounters specify minimum limits of sales turnover. Venture capitalists have minimum limits on the amounts of money which they are prepared to invest.

   Managers of clearing banks have maximum limits above which they are not permitted to lend. The customer is not aware of these maximum limits but they are related to the status of the branch.

6 *Supporting information.* There is no agreement amongst financiers about the information which is expected to accompany an application for financial assistance. It is often not known in advance whether a comprehensive twenty-page plan (see 98) or a single broadsheet is initially needed and whether an opportunity will be given to provide supplementary information if that initially provided is inadequate.

7 *Communication.* This is a difficulty for both sides in negotiations and applications. Financiers use terms which

are not in the business manager's usual vocabulary. (The Glossary defines a number of them.) On the other hand small business managers have in-depth knowledge, often on a technical nature, which it is difficult to translate into meaningful non-technical prose.

8 *Requirement for collateral.* When assets are mortgaged, subject to hire purchase and leasing, the designated goods are the collateral so there is less difficulty than when the finance is needed for unspecified activities related to the general use of working capital. Financiers need to be assured that they can use the collateral which has been pledged to recover their money should a business fail and be unable to redeem its debts.

Family houses and insurance policies, provided they are worth enough are required as collateral. Insurance policies can be covered by 'key person' insurance but people with families may be unwilling to risk losing their home if a business fails. Companies may have to agree to fixed and floating charges on their assets. This difficulty is especially detrimental to young people who have had no time to accumulate collateral or to match advances from financiers with equivalent amounts of their own money.

9 *Competition for funds.* Financiers are approached not only by small businesses but also by medium and large ones. They may have attractive propositions, good track records, requirements for large amounts of money with good earnings potential for a financier. The administration may be little more than is needed when managing funds and facilities granted to small businesses.

10 *Setting up and preparation charges.* These apply to the majority of facilities granted by financiers. Clearing banks may charge for a manager's time spent in arranging a facility for a small business. Surveyor's, valuer's and solicitor's fees have to be paid.

The following table shows some typical charges of a venture capitalist:

Amount advanced £	Charge £	Commission %
10,000	500	5
20,000	900	4.5
30,000	1,200	4
40,000	1,400	3.5
50,000	1,500	3
60,000	1,600	2.7
70,000	1,700	2.4

If a business advertises for financial assistance the cost of the advertisement is an additional cost. If accountants are needed to assist with the preparation of a plan they too have to be paid. There is also the hidden cost of the small business manager's time involved in preparation and negotiation. That investment of time and money must be seen against the possibility of the application being declined so the time and money spent in preparation may be lost.

11 *Changes in government policy.* These changes percolate through the financial chain and eventually affect the supply of credit to businesses. The amount of money available and/or its cost can be affected.

12 *Changes in personnel.* Once a facility has been agreed changes in personnel occupying management posts in the financial institutions can affect relationships with small businesses. New managers cannot be relied upon to behave in a manner identical to their predecessors. They need time to familiarize themselves with their customers.

Financiers' expectations

All these difficulties should not be regarded as awkwardness on the part of financiers. As with any business they too expect to profit from their activities and avoid loss-making activities. They expect:

1 To see evidence that personal guarantees given to support overdrafts and loans can be honoured by the guarantor. Questions are therefore asked about the financial standing

of the guarantor: savings, income, property, share-holdings, life insurance policies and the amount paid against them.

2   To be assured that the debts can be serviced should a facility be granted.

3   To earn an attractive rate of return and payment for services rendered (e.g. setting up a facility) or ultimately to make a capital gain.

Financiers' sanctions

After a business has located and agreed a source of external funds the difficulties have not ended. The confidence of the financier has to be retained and obligations honoured by the business. If a business fails to do this the financier begins by giving polite warnings which, if they do not produce an acceptable response, may result in sanctions being applied.

Clearing banks can refuse to pay cheques, standing orders and direct debits. A supplementary charge may be levied on the business to pay for the bank's time. Overdrafts can be called in and personal guarantees demanded. Collateral may be sold. Alternatively a bank may put a company into liquidation.

Other financiers may call in loans or refuse previously agreed draw-down facilities. Besides being confronted by the financiers' sanctions, a business may find disquiet amongst suppliers and collectors of rates and taxes if news of liquidity problems reaches them.

Overcoming the difficulties

Although there are difficulties associated with introducing external money into a business, there are enough success stories to demonstrate that they are not insuperable. Success cannot, of course, be guaranteed but the following points are relevant:

1   Carry out desk-top *research* on the opportunities available. This involves reading the financial press, searching

directories, contacting advertisers (initially by telephone to save time and money), enlisting the help of accountants, avoiding unnecessary travel and relating the possible sources of external finance to one's own business situation.

2   Adopt a resilient *attitude*. If the first financier declines an application for assistance, the next one may make a positive response.

3   Acquire an acceptable *track record* either personally or for the business.

4   Acquire *collateral* in anticipation of it being needed, but do not volunteer it. It is not unknown for a facility to be as little as 10 per cent of the market value of the collateral pledged as security for it.

5   Cover any collateral with *insurance*.

6   Avoid being obligated to a *single source* of finance. Many managers choose to have their personal and business accounts at different banks. Two small businesses with the same management team may choose not to have the accounts of both businesses with the same bank.

   If possible external finance should come from different sources, e.g. leases, overdrafts and loans.

7   *Fulfil obligations* to financiers and remember that they have provided a service.

8   Use the accounting and financial systems of the business to provide *control information* for monitoring the situation and flagging emergencies before they become crises.

9   Be realistic when making *forecasts*. Events outside the control of the business can always make forecasts unrealistic so the manager should not make them even more unrealistic.

14 The utilization of surpluses

From time to time a small business may already have or expect to have money which is surplus to requirements. After requirements for working capital, designated expenditure and obligations to creditors have been met, the business may be in the happy position of having to decide what to do with the surplus. Should it be retained in the business or lent/invested to a person or institution outside the business?

Decisions associated with the use and/or disposal of the surplus involve the evaluation of short and long term opportunities, policies and the strategic plans of the business.

The surplus can take different forms. It may be a single one-off lump sum. On the other hand, it may be a series of surpluses of different amounts of money spreading, maybe irregularly, over a long period of time. Some of the latter surpluses may be the subject of some conjecture.

Before the opportunities (be they external or internal) can be evaluated within the business the following information is needed:

1 The amount of the surplus or surpluses if there is more than one.
2 When it or they will become available.
3 The length of time for which the money will be available.

Budgets and financial plans should be of some assistance in providing this information.

Borrowers' principles and practices

Exhibit 14.1 summarizes typical investment opportunities. Underlying this information are certain principles. The amount of interest paid reflects the duration of the investment, the magnitude of the risk and an estimate by financial institutions of the way interest rates will behave during the lifetime of the investment. The most secure investments have the lowest rates of interest because the possibility of the borrower being unable to repay the lender is so remote as to be negligible.

The investments with highest risk hold out the possibility of the highest return on investment. The possibility of losing all or part of the money invested at high risk however must be recognized. Many financial advisers therefore recommend a spread or portfolio of investments as a precaution against losing everything.

Investors who are prepared to lend their money for long periods earn higher rates of interest than those who choose investments with minimal notice of withdrawal.

Intermediaries between lenders and borrowers, (brokers, agents and fund managers), may be prepared to give advice to lenders besides handling the actual investment if the borrower requires the participation of an intermediary. Exhibit 14.1 shows a number of investment opportunities where there is no participation by an intermediary. Intermediaries have scales of charges which may state a minimum amount of money which they are prepared to handle for a client. There may be a minimum charge and thereafter a pro rata charge which gradually decreases as the amount of money increases.

Organizations and institutions which accept money for investment, be it from businesses or individuals, have their own requirements for the efficient management of their own business. Consequently lenders and depositors are expected to comply with the borrowers' terms. Compliance means that, for example, if a deposited investment is withdrawn before the end of its term, a penalty has to be paid. There are however many investments which do not have maturity dates.

The effects of market forces

All investments are in some measure affected by market forces whether or not they have maturity dates. Bank interest rates, quoted shares, the money market, commodities and future markets react quickly to any changes. The effect on a business

Exhibit 14.1 *Summary of investment objectives and opportunities*

Investment opportunities (Stable (St) or Speculative (Sp)):

- Own business (Sp)
- Bank — Current A/c (St)
- Bank — Deposit A/c (St)
- Building Society — Fixed term fixed % (St)
- Building Society — Variable % (St)
- Traded on SE — Government stocks / Shares (Sp)
- Shares (Sp)
- Government stocks (St)
- Unit trusts — Income (Sp)
- Unit trusts — Capital growth (Sp)
- Money markets (Sp)
- Futures (Sp)
- Buy property for leasing and rental (Sp)
- Buy objets d'arts (Sp)
- Pension fund topping up (St)
- Endowment insurances (St)
- Venture capital (Sp)

Investment objectives:

- Stable (St) or Speculative (Sp)
- Easy accessibility withdrawal
  - no notice
  - short notice
  - medium
  - long
  - difficult
- Interest
  - no early withdrawal penalty
  - fixed
  - Regular intervals
  - variable from 0%
  - Continuously credited
  - variable
  - Potentially high but uncertain
- Maximum security
- Avoidance of management fees and commissions
- Capital gain possible
- Maximum control of investment
- Minimum delay in crediting cheques
- Spread of investments
- No minimum

Key
X Usual situation
O Occasional situation

may be considerable and may necessitate some difficult decisions to avoid money being lost. If prices fall should the business 'get out quickly' or 'keep its nerve' and do nothing until the direction the market is taking becomes a little clearer? On the other hand if prices rise should a business sell or should it wait for the price to rise even higher?

Judgement is needed. Apart from their effects on prices being offered for the various types of investment opportunities, there is another effect. That is the effect on a business whereby a constant call on management time is made. If that time is not available, the choice for investing surpluses is reduced to two. First there are the low key external ones, like bank deposits with stable but unspectacular rates of interest. Secondly, there is the opportunity to invest in the business itself.

Investing in the business

Exhibit 14.1 shows the disadvantages associated with investing in one's own business. Success is dependent on the management of the business having the requisite skills. As it is a small business it is less equipped to resist the effects of unfavourable market forces. Moreover, once money has been committed, it may be difficult to release it for other uses until such a time as it earns the income for which it was primarily and initially invested.

There are however considerable advantages. There are no fees or commissions to be paid unless an estate agent is used to let property built for letting and leasing. There is no reliance on third parties to provide information. Accurate information is much more likely from one's own business given adequate reporting procedures and management information.

Exhibit 14.2 summarizes the opportunities which are available to a business which chooses to invest or 'plough back' surpluses in whole or in part.

The above examples are invariably subject to non-financial constraints. There are many examples of such constraints. There may not be storage space available for the stock if it were acquired, sufficient or suitable businesses and patents for sale or workers coming forward for employment in, for them, a new business.

Exhibit 14.2 *Summary of opportunities for investment in the business itself ('ploughing back')*

Type of opportunity	*Examples*
Acquisition of:	Current assets, e.g. stock to give: (*a*) better service and shorter manufacturing lead times (*b*) anticipation of price increases Intangible assets: patents, licences, franchises Other businesses for product and market diversification, increased sales volumes so as to decrease unit costs Fixed assets: purchase of premises and plant from existing owners, if they are prepared to sell what is currently leased or rented. Buy new premises for own use or for letting
Improvements in:	Manufacturing methods: new tooling, changes in layouts, use of consultants new equipment Public relations: donations and sponsorship Industrial relations: profit sharing, working conditions Capital structure: capitalization of reserves Cash reserves Composition of workforce: recruitment of personnel with new skills Premises: refurbishment

Development of:	Personnel: training in management, methods, new equipment
	Products: incorporation of state of the art improvements, new lines
	Markets: advertising, visits overseas, additional sales personnel, market research
Wealth distribution to:	Employees: wage and salary increases, bonus shares, pension rights
	Ordinary shareholders: dividend increases, scrip issues

After applying these non-financial constraints a short list of opportunities for investment in the business is prepared by a process of elimination. The opportunities remaining may then be evaluated before a decision to proceed is taken.

The funds available are then allocated by a budgeting or supplementary financial planning exercise to those opportunities. It is unlikely that sufficient funds will be available to take up all the opportunities.

Conclusion

If investment in the opportunities is properly managed the result will be a strengthening of the net worth of the business.

Part Four   Glossary of terms

The manager of a small business encounters a wide range of different financial terms. Owing to the size of the business many of these terms are not part of his or her everyday working vocabulary. This glossary of terms has been prepared so that the manager may have available definitions of terms which may be unfamiliar and, in addition, those which are frequently used but seldom defined.

Absorption costing A method of costing where all costs are identified with (that is, absorbed by) units of output and stock. Thus all costs of a particular period are allocated between that period's output and the stocks in hand at the end of the period.

Acceptance house A financial institution accessed via a clearing bank which accepts bills of exchange as security for lending money at a discounted rate. The acceptance house may not itself lend money but may sign the bill and pass it to another institution which specializes in lending.

Accountancy The practice of: (a) Counting and recording income and expenditure of the business and its constituent sections for internal and external use; (b) Translating the activities of the business into monetary terms; (c) Explaining the performance of the constituent sections of the business; (d) Supporting the financial manager and, in the absence of such a person, discharging the duties of financial management.

Accumulated depreciation The total amount written off since an asset was acquired.

Accrual The amount of current expenditure properly set off against current income but not yet paid for at the end of the accountancy period.

Acid test A measure of liquidity in the short term obtained by solving the equation: Cash + negotiable instruments + debtors : Current liabilities. A figure in excess of 0.8 is preferred by credit controllers.

Act of God In insurance, an event arising directly and exclusively from natural causes without human intervention which could not have been prevented by any amount of foresight, pains or care reasonably to have been expected.

Actuary A person primarily associated with life insurance who assesses statistically, by trend study, mortality rates for the calculation of life premiums and the management of pension funds. The actuary applies theories of mathematical probability, compound interest and other statistical models, e.g. investment management and risk models.

Administrator   In the specialist sense, a person appointed by the court to assist with the reorganization of a company in difficulties where there are reasonable prospects of a return to profitability or more advantageous use of assets.

Aged debtor analysis   An analysis of customers (debtors) owing money beyond the stated credit terms of the supplier and the length of time overdue.

Agent   A person vested with authority to act for a business or person. (For example, freight, insurance, commission, sales, purchasing agents.)

Airway bill   A document issued by an airline describing the goods, the departure airport, destination, time of departure, flight details and responsibility for payment of charges.

All risks insurance   All risks of physical loss or damage which in addition to fire and additional perils includes any accidental damage or loss not specifically excluded. The exclusions (e.g. wear and tear, electrical and mechanical breakdown, gradual deterioration) are specifically stated in the policy. Certain other 'property' risks (e.g. theft, goods in transit and money) may be added or incorporated into the cover. An excess is normally applied to all covers except fire, explosion, earthquake, riot, aircraft and money.

Alpha share   The most marketable share of those traded on the Stock Exchange.

Amortization   A reduction in debt by periodic payments covering interest and principal so as to write off the cost of a tangible asset over a period of years.

Annuity   A fixed sum of money payable in equal amounts following a certain event (e.g. retirement) usually for an unlimited period of time. Annuities may be purchased at the end of a period of contributions to a pension fund.

Apportionment   *See* Cost allocation.

Appreciation   The opposite of depreciation. Some assets of a business increase in value with the passage of time.

Articles of association   The regulations governing the internal affairs of a limited company. The articles specify the rights, duties and powers of the members of the company together with the powers of the directors.

Assets Everything a business owns or is due to it. (a) *Current assets*: cash, short term deposits, debtors, stocks of raw materials, work in progress and finished stocks. (b) *Fixed assets*: buildings and machinery. (c) *Intangible assets*: patents, designs, goodwill.

Asset backing The assets of a company: land, stocks, cash, buildings, machinery and intangible property.

Asset turnover The ratio of sales to assets employed in the business. An increase in the ratio implies a more efficient use.

Assurance The term used to relate exclusively to life assurance but nowadays the terms assurance and insurance are interchanged. The term 'insurance' is used for all perils and tends to predominate, although 'assurance' still appears in the names of a number of insurers.

Auditor The person who examines the records of a business and gives an opinion on their accuracy. There is a legal obligation for the accounts of a limited company to be audited by a member of certain specified accounting bodies.

Avalize The practice whereby a foreign customers' bank endorses a negotiable instrument (e.g. a bill of exchange) and thus guarantees payment to the supplier.

Back-to-back credit A credit given by a finance house acting as an intermediary between a foreign buyer and a foreign seller.

Bad debt A debt which cannot be recovered and has to be treated as a loss.

Bailiff An officer empowered by a court to service writs and recover property.

Bank An institution whose business is handling other people's money.

Bank account The record of money (a) paid into (cash, cheques, documentary credits, transfers, direct debits) and (b) withdrawals from the account leaving either a credit or debit balance.

Current accounts usually do not earn interest but may attract charges according to the number of transactions or period of time covered by a statement, renewal of a facility, bank manager's time, amount of credit balance, penalties for unauthorized use of the account and standing charges. They do not require notice for authorized withdrawals. *Deposit accounts* earn interest but require notice of withdrawals. *Loan accounts* and *escrow accounts* (qv).

Bank advance   A loan of a fixed amount by a bank usually against security. The amount is fixed and interest is payable at an agreed rate.

Bank buying rate   The rate at which a bank agrees to buy a specified amount of currency in exchange for another currency.

Bank draft   *See* Draft.

Bank overdraft   An arrangement whereby the debit balance on a current account can reach an agreed borrowing limit. Interest is payable but the rate fluctuates.

Bank selling rate   The rate at which a bank agrees to sell to its customers a specified amount of one currency in exchange for another.

Bankruptcy   A method of relieving businesses and individuals of their overburdening debts in return for which they have to suffer certain disabilities (e.g., severe restrictions on the availability of credit).

Barter   The exchange of goods of one type for those of another often with a merchant bank acting as an intermediary.

Bear   Someone who thinks the stock market or a particular share will go down. A bear market is one in which the majority of share prices are falling due to a predominance of sellers.

Bed and breakfast   The practice of selling shares one day and buying the share next day to minimize capital gains tax.

Beta share   The second of the grades of marketability of the Stock Exchange Automated Quotation System.

Bill of exchange   An unconditional order in writing (a) Addressed by one person or business (e.g. a supplier) to another person or business (e.g. a customer); (b) Signed by the person giving it on the face and reverse. (c) Requiring the person to whom it is addressed to (*i*) pay on demand or (*ii*) at a fixed or determinable future time or to the order of the drawer or bearer.

If there is any doubt about the possible unwillingness of the addressee signing, *irrevocable letters of credit* should be substituted for bills of exchange. The bill may be drawn on company letterhead or on a preprinted form.

Bill of lading   A document usually issued in connection with the carriage of goods by sea. It states: (a) the name and address of the customer; (b) a description of goods and (c) shipping details. Copies are distributed by the carrier to (a) the supplier of the goods; (b) the shipping agent; (c) the customer or the customer's agent so that the goods may be claimed.

Blocked funds Money due from customers which because of government intervention in the country concerned cannot be transferred to the supplier, at least not for the foreseeable future.

Blue chip share An ordinary share of a very substantial company on the Stock Exchange.

Bond (1) A written promise to pay the holder a sum of money at a certain date more than one year after the issue at a stated annual rate of interest.

(2) The place where dutiable goods are held.

(3) An undertaking by a third party to pay out should the person or business guaranteed by the bond default. For example, bond entered into by businesses who have an arrangement with Customs and Excise whereby VAT payable on imports is deferred.

Bookkeeping Keeping the accounts of a business.

Book value (1) The book value of an ordinary share in a company is determined from the company's records by (a) adding all assets (although intangible assets such as goodwill are usually excluded); (b) deducting debts and other liabilities plus the liquidation price of any preference share; (c) The sum arrived at is divided by the number of ordinary shares outstanding. This is also known as the *net asset value* of a share.

(2) The value at which an asset is recorded in the accounts of a business.

Borrowing The temporary use of money. The sum borrowed (the *principal*) usually has to be returned with interest. Banks often charge for setting up a borrowing facility.

Break even The original definition as illustrated on charts assumed linear relationships and defined it as the level of output or value of sales (revenue) where total costs equal total revenue. The availability of computerized calculating facilities has refined break even analysis so that it is possible to have two break even points: a lower one, as before, and an upper one beyond which costs again exceed revenue.

These can apply to businesses which supply perishable goods with a limited shelf life to markets which become saturated so goods have to be 'sold off' or disposed of. The linear gradient line representing costs on these break even charts is unchanged. As more goods are produced costs continue to rise. However the revenue or income is represented by a curved line. After intersecting the linear costs line, it continues to rise to an optimum point from whence it starts to double back on itself until it again intersects the costs line. As it falls away goods have to be sold or disposed of at a loss. Between the upper and lower points there is a *profit envelope*.

Broker   An intermediary who (a) makes contracts without having the goods or documents of title (e.g. insurance policy, airway bill, bill of lading) and (b) receives a commission.

Budget   A financial or quantitative statement of the desired or intended activity of a business for a stated future period (e.g. one year).

Budget variance   The difference between actual costs incurred in an operation and the costs expected when the plan was made.

Bull   Someone who thinks the stockmarket or a certain share will go up in price.

Business interruption   A type of insurance designed to protect a business against reduced earnings following insured damage (see page 127).

Buy-out   The transfer of ownership of a business from a large corporation or company to its current managers, also called a 'management buy-out'.

Call   Money due on partly paid securities.

Call option   The right to buy (a futures market term).

Capacity costs   Those costs necessary in order to provide the operational assets and organization to be ready to manufacture and sell the related goods, up to a planned maximum volume of output.

Capital budgeting   Planning for future capital expenditure. It involves (a) the forecasting of initial outlays; (b) the financing of those outlays; and (c) the expected future cash flow effects.

Capital employed   There is no universally accepted definition. It is defined as (a) capital invested for the long term or (b) long life assets plus working capital (those assets of shorter lives) see page 22.

Capitalization The total amount of various securities issued by a company. Capitalization may include loan stock, preference and ordinary shares.

Cash budget A schedule of expected cash receipts and payments during a stated future period.

Cash discount The reduction given by a supplier when an account is paid before a specified date.

Cash flow The net income of a business plus non–cash charges (e.g. depreciation and charges to reserves). *Gross cash flow* and *net cash flow* respectively relate to the pre- and post-tax net incomes plus non-cash charges.

Certificate of insurance A document issued by an insurer as evidence that the premium has been paid and the policy to which it refers is in force.

Certificate of posting A document issued at the time of posting acknowledging that a stated letter or parcel has been handed over for posting.

Charge card An embossed plastic card which enables the holder to authorize a supplier of goods and services to charge the cost to a named account.

Charges forward The buyer or customer pays for the cost of carriage and agent's charges when the goods are received at their destination.

Chartism A method of investment whereby the share price patterns on charts are interpreted for an indication of future share price trends.

Cheque A written order to a banker to pay a specified sum of money to a named person or business. A crossed cheque may only be paid into a bank account. Cheques payable to a limited company cannot be used to pay a third party. Cheques payable to unincorporated businesses may be endorsed on the reverse by the drawee and used to pay third parties.

Cleared balance Money in a bank account which has passed through the banks' clearing system.

Clearing bank A High Street bank which receives cheques from its customers and passes them to a central point for processing (a clearing house). The clearing houses sets off amounts owed between banks so that only one sum is paid by a debtor bank to a creditor bank.

Collateral   Securities other than property (e.g. stocks, shares, insurance policies, land and buildings) pledged by a borrower to secure repayment of a loan or overdraft.

Commission   A payment to an intermediary (e.g. an agent or broker) for services rendered.

Comptroller   One of the names used instead of financial manager or financial director.

Compulsory liquidation   A creditor unable to obtain payment of a debt presents a petition or request to the court for winding up the debtor company.

Confirming house   A type of export house which acts for an overseas buyer. An order is played on a UK supplier on behalf of a foreign buyer and all the arrangements made for payment to the supplier.

Confirmed irrevocable letter of credit   An irrevocable letter of credit which is confirmed by a British bank. (*See* Irrevocable letter of credit and Letter of credit.)

Conservatism   The practice whereby prudent financial managers do not anticipate gains as yet unrealized but provide for all losses which have arisen or are likely to arise.

Consideration   The cost of a purchase or proceeds of a sale before the addition of commission and other charges.

Consistency   An accounting convention. Where there are alternative, acceptable methods of calculating or treating specific terms in the accounts, the method actually chosen and operated should be used consistently. Without consistency comparisons between sets of accounts are meaningless.

Consumable material   Material which is generally consumed in the course of manufacture and not directly attributable to a particular product.

Continuous budget   A method of budgeting which continually covers a specific future period (e.g. one year). At the end of a period, a month or quarter, or a period equivalent in duration to the one just passed, is added to the end of the budget.

Contribution   The amount by which sales exceed variable (i.e. direct income).

Controllable cost   A cost which may be directly regulated or influenced by action at a given level of managerial authority.

Conversion   The process of translating £s from a historical basis to figures which reflect their current purchasing power.

Convertible (1) A *debenture* which may be exchanged by the owner for ordinary shares or another security of the same company in accordance with the terms of issue.

(2) A *currency* which may be exchanged into another currency at a published rate of exchange.

Cost allocation or **apportionment** The assignment or allotment of proportions of the total overhead costs of a business to one or more cost centres in accordance with either (a) the benefits received or (b) the responsibilities to other cost centres.

Costing The methods and means by which relevant costs of processes and products are ascertained.

Cost of sales The total costs incurred in selling (i.e., promotion and distribution).

Counter trade An arrangement whereby an exporter or exporting country has to accept goods from the importer or importing country.

Cover (1) The relationship between dividend paid and the profits available for payment.

(2) The amount insured.

Court receivership When a partnership dispute occurs, and in some other circumstances, application can be made to the court for the appointment of a *receiver*.

Creative accounting A controversial practice which pushes accounting rules to their limits of acceptability to create a wealthy state of financial affairs in the accounts.

Credit agency An organization which (a) verifies the creditworthiness of a potential customer; (b) collects overdue debts on behalf of a supplier.

Credit card An embossed plastic card issued by a specialist financial organization which enables the holder to obtain goods or services on credit up to a pre-arranged limit from participating suppliers. After a certain date the amount outstanding attracts interest.

Credit insurance An arrangement whereby exporting businesses may insure against the risks of non-payment by their customers.

Credit note A document issued by a supplier giving credit for goods returned or invoicing mistakes.

Credit payment A payment into a bank account.

Credit rating The reputation of a business for payment of monies due on time and in the required amounts.

Credit sale   Goods or services supplied to a customer who has an arrangement for paying the supplier at a date after the goods or service were received.

Credit score   A numerical expression of creditworthiness.

Creditor   One to whom money is owed.

Cross rate   The rate of exchange between two non–sterling currencies.

Crossed cheque   A cheque which must be paid into a bank.

Currency swap   An arrangement for eliminating exchange risks.

Current account   *See* Bank account.

Current assets   The assets which are expected to be realized in cash if sold or consumed during the normal operating cycle of the business. These include cash, debtors, short term investments and all forms of stock. They are frequently called *circulating assets* because they are or should be on the move (e.g. from raw material to finished goods to cash or from wholesale purchases to retail sales to cash).

Current liabilities   Money owed and payable by a business. Items due within one year may also be classified as current liabilities.

Current ratio   An index of liquidity or creditworthiness derived by dividing the book value of the total current assets by the book value of the total current liabilities. An indication of short-term ability to pay (the *quick ratio* (qv) does not include stock).

Debenture   A written acknowledgement of a debt owing by a business. Normally the document is under seal. The debt carries a fixed rate of interest and is repayable within a fixed number of years. The debt is usually secured by assets of the business or its executives but it may be unsecured.

Debtor   One who owes money.

Deed of arrangement   Individuals in financial trouble can arrange with their creditors for their assets to be put into the hands of a trustee for distribution to creditors. The disabilities of bankruptcy are thereby avoided.

Deposit   (1) Money paid to a supplier as part or all of the money for goods to be supplied. This practice is colloquially known as 'putting money up front'.

(2) A bank account which earns more interest than a current account.

Demerger   The opposite of a merger, that is the separation of two businesses which were formerly amalgamated.

Depreciation   Charges against earnings to write off the cost less the salvage (resale) value of a fixed asset over its useful life. It is an accounting entry and does not represent a cash outlay nor are any funds earmarked for the purpose.

Deviation   A marine insurance term used when a ship or aircraft deviates from its course without prejudicing the policy.

Dilution   A reduction in earnings per share resulting from an increase in ordinary share capital or through a *scrip issue*.

Direct costing   Charging all direct costs (variable materials, labour and expenses) which enter into and are embodied in the finished product. *Note.* Some so-called fixed costs may be regarded as variable costs in certain circumstances (repairs and maintenance, tools etc) and thus be included in the *variable costs* of manufacture.

Direct debit   A payment/collection system whereby, subject to prior permission being given and adequate safe-guards being in place, a supplier may debit the current bank account of a customer without first seeking the permission of the customer and raising an invoice. The customer does not have to draw a cheque.

Direct labour costs   Expenditure on labour which is directly attributable to a product or activity.

Direct material   Expenditure on material which is incorporated into the finished product.

Directors' and officers' liability cover   A form of insurance to cover proven negligence but not malpractice in the event of a company being wound up.

Director   A member of the managing board who directs, rules and guides.

Disclosure letter   A document used when selling a business to inform the purchaser of any matters which if undisclosed could lead to subsequent claims under warranties and indemnities.

Discount   The precise definition depends on the context. The basic idea present in all the different contexts is that of reducing what is due. (1) A share may be at a discount, i.e. below its normal price.
   (2) The price of goods and services may be reduced because

(a) cash is paid or payment is made before a due date, i.e., a cash discount or (b) the volume of sales is such as to justify a quantity discount.

Discount bond   A device used for lending money to a company. There is little or no income but it rolls up to give a substantial repayment.

Discount house   An organization which discounts bills of exchange sent to it by clearing banks.

Discounted cash flow   A group of methods of capital expenditure evaluation *viz* (1) yield; (2) net present value; (3) annual value. An interest discounting factor is applied to the forecast returns on the investment. This has the effect of levying a rate of interest charge on each year's budgeted cash receipts.

Disincorporation   The name given to the process whereby a limited company voluntarily reverts to partnership or sole trader status.

Distraint   A remedy available to a creditor, e.g. rent due to a landlord. The creditor can enter the debtor's premises, seize property and retain it until the debt is paid with the authority of the court.

Dividend   A regular payment by a company to its shareholders normally out of earnings.

Dividend cover   The number of times that earnings cover the net cost of the dividend. Those dividends with the highest cover are the most secure.

Double taxation relief   The arrangement whereby earnings taxed in a foreign country are not taxed at the full rate in the UK.

Doubtful debt   An overdue sum of money where recovery is unlikely.

Draft   (1) A document issued by a bank only when payment is made in advance. Travellers cheques are one form of bank draft.

(2) Bills of exchange are sometimes referred to as drafts.

Earnings   The amount of profit available for ordinary shareholders.

Earnings per share   Earnings divided by the number of issued ordinary shares.

Earnings yield   Earnings per share expressed as a percentage of the share price.

Employer's liability insurance   A category of insurance cover which is mandatory on employers so as to provide for risks associated with their employees.

Encumbered   Property or assets which are mortgaged or pledged as security. The opposite is *unencumbered*.

Endorsement   A term used in connection with *bills of exchange* and *cheques* whereby the recipient signs the reverse so that they may be negotiated. Cheques payable to limited companies cannot be negotiated.

Equity   The face value of ordinary shares.

Escrow   A bank account or contract which is dependent upon a certain condition being met.

Euro currency   A deposit in any major market currency held outside the country which issued the currency.

Exchange rate   The equivalent value of the £ Sterling in the currency of another country.

Exercise price or **strike price**   The price at which the options buyer (holder) has the right to buy or sell the underlying futures contract.

Exit   A generic term referring to the disposal of a business (e.g. the sale of a company on the retirement of a director).

Exit PE   The P/E ratio calculation is the price offered to shareholders when a takeover bid is made.

Exotics   A foreign exchange dealers' term for currencies for which there is only a small market.

Ex-works   A term used in connection with the price of goods to emphasize that carriage, agents' and tax charges are excluded.

Factoring   A form of sales invoice discounting involving assigning the debts to a named *factor*. The factor accepts responsibility for all or some of the sales ledger functions, *viz.* debt collection and credit control. In addition the factor arranges for a business to draw money against the assigned debts up to a prearranged limit (e.g. 70% at a premium rate of interest) before the customers have paid the factor for the supplier's goods or services.

Factory cost   The cost of manufacturing a product. Prime costs (labour and materials) are included, but costs associated with selling are excluded.

Factory overhead   All factory costs other than direct labour, direct materials and direct expenses.

Fictitious assets   Expenditure not charged to the profit and loss account of the year in which it occurred. The relevant amounts are shown in the balance sheets until written off to the profit and loss appropriation accounts in future years to achieve more realistic matching of income with expenditure.

Finance   The pecuniary resources of a business.

Finance house   A company whose business is speculative lending.

Fire insurance   A form of contract in which the insurer, in return for a payment of a premium, undertakes to indemnify the insured against the consequences of fire, lightning and domestic explosion as stated in the policy subject to the adequacy of the sums insured. A fire must comprise actual ignition and be fortuitous in origin. As required additional perils may be added to this contract (e.g., fuel explosion, earthquake, riot and civil commotion, malicious damage, aircraft damage, storm, tempest and flood, bursting and overflowing water apparatus, impact by third party vehicles, cattle or impact by the insured's own vehicles, sprinkler leakage and even in certain circumstances risk such as falling trees, leakage of fuel oil). The policy states the full risk of each perit granted. Excesses are usually applied to malicious damage, all water damage and impact by the insured's own vehicles.

Firm quotation   A quotation relating to a foreign exchange rate at which a bank is prepared to deal as opposed to a quotation which is for information only.

Fiscal year   The government's financial year.

Fixed assets   The capital expenditure of a business in respect of its permanent or semi-permanent physical structure. These possessions are not held for resale but are retained to assist with earning income for the business.

Fixed charges   A type of business expense which cannot be easily identified with a specific output. Such expenses do not vary generally with output unless there are major changes.

Fixed costs   A cost, which for a particular capacity structure, does not change in total during a given period. However fixed costs per unit of sale or manufacture vary with output.

Fixed forward contract   *See* Forward contract.

Flexible budget   A budget that is prepared for a range of possible activity levels and not for a single level of activity. It is usually related only to overhead costs. Variable materials and labour may also be included.

Forecast   A conjectural estimate of something future.

Forfaiting   A merchant bank, known as a *Forfaitist* buys from an exporter *promissory notes* payable by a foreign purchaser of capital goods over a medium period (e.g. one to seven years).

Forgery   Counterfeiting or falsifying a document.

Forward contract   A legally binding contract between a bank and a customer. The customer agrees to receive or deliver foreign currency at a pre-arranged exchange rate and time or within a specified period. No money is exchanged at the time the contract is taken out.

Forward cover   The arrangement of a foreign exchange contract to protect a buyer or seller of a foreign currency at a future date from unexpected adverse fluctuations in the exchange rate.

Franchise   A contract between a *franchisor* and a *franchisee*. The franchisor owns the rights to a branded product, concept or service. In return for a payment, the franchisee acquires the right to the intellectual and physical property of the franchisor in a designated sales area and to receive promotional support. A franchisor, sometimes called a 'mother company', is more involved in the day-to-day support of the franchisee than is the case with the licensor–licensee and principal–agent contractual relationships.

Franked investment income   Investment income from which tax has been deducted.

Fraud   Deceitfulness, criminal deception and making use of false representations.

Full listing   A quotation on the Stock Exchange.

Future   Forward sales or forward purchases of commodities, stocks and shares usually for speculation.

Gamma share   The least marketable of the three gradings on the Stock Exchange Automated Quotation System.

Garnishee order   An order by a court to a creditor restraining a debtor from disposing of property until a sum of money to clear the debts has been paid to the creditor.

Gearing   The ratio between (a) the issued preference share and debentures, and (b) the issued ordinary shares. (The various shares and debentures are expressed in nominal share values). It can indicate that a company is too dependent on external finances.

Gilts   Government stocks.

Golden shares   A share which cannot be freely sold except to specified categories of buyers.

Grant   A donation usually of money to assist with a specific venture.

Guarantor   One who acts as surety for a debt.

Hire purchase   An agreement whereby regular hire charges are paid over an agreed period. At the end of the period the ownership of the property is transferred in the same way as when the property is purchased.

Historical costing   The ascertainment of the cost of some activity by reference to costs which have already been incurred.

Holding gain (or loss)   The difference between the value to a business of an asset and the (depreciated) initial acquisition cost incurred by the business in purchasing that asset.

Holiday   A prior arrangement whereby capital or interest is deferred to be repaid at the end of an agreed period.

Ideal output   The maximum number of items which could be produced in a given period with a given physical capacity, no allowance being made for any form of production stoppage.

Ideal standard   The standard cost and efficiency performance which can be attained under the most favourable conditions possible, no allowance being made for any form of production stoppage.

Incoterms   International rules for the interpretation of trade terms.

Incremental costs   The difference between the total costs of two alternative courses of action.

Index   An indication of prices related to a base line of 100.

Index linking   Payments connected to a named index (e.g. Retail Price Index) and some pension schemes.

Indirect labour cost   Any expenditure on labour which is not directly attributable to the product being manufactured.

Insolvency   An inability to pay debts as they become due.

Institutional investor   A financial organization which handles investments on behalf of others (e.g. insurance companies, pension funds, unit trusts).

Insurance   A contract on speculation.

Intangible assets   Those assets which cannot be seen or touched although they may have some value (e.g. patents, trade marks, copyrights and goodwill).

Interest   The amount of money paid by a borrower to a lender in return for a loan or overdraft, credit card or hire purchase agreement. The interest may be fixed or variable.

Interest rate swap   An arrangement for eliminating interest rate risks.

Internal audit   The audit conducted by the business itself with a view to ensuring that systems to secure assets and possessions (e.g. against fraud) are being maintained.

Internal check   The self-regulatory methods and procedures in a business which operate continuously in checking day-to-day transactions as a matter of routine.

Internal control   A series of systems and checking procedures designed to achieve maximum accuracy and minimize fraud.

Investigation   A detailed assessment of the financial situation of a business.

Investment company   A company which uses its funds to acquire shares or securities.

Investment trust   A public limited company with a fixed number of shares whose business is buying and selling shares in the Stock Exchange.

Inventory   Stocks: raw materials, unfinished and finished.

Invoice discounting   The practice of obtaining money on the security of book debts.

Irrevocable letter of credit   A documentary credit which cannot be cancelled or altered without the agreement of the buyer and seller. A *confirmed irrevocable letter* is one which will be paid even if the buyer or foreign bank is unable to pay. The supplier has to comply with its terms and provide specified documents (e.g. negotiable documents and non-negotiable documents, bills of exchange (drafts), airway bills, bills of lading, advice notes, certificates of origin issued by a chamber of commerce, certificates of insurance).

Job costing   A method of apportioning manufacturing costs to specific single orders. Computer software is available for doing this.

Key person insurance   *See* Term insurance.

Labour efficiency variances   The difference between the actual hours expended and the standard hours specified multiplied by the standard rate for the work.

Lease   A means of financing the use of an asset. The lessee is not the owner but has full use of the asset. A leasing company purchases the capital asset or property and rents it to the business which uses it.

Leaseback   An arrangement whereby a business sells an asset to a leasing company and then takes out a lease on it. The asset does not physically move although the ownership is transferred.

Letter of credit   A foreign buyer arranges with a bank to open a credit in the country of the seller. On presentation of the relevant shipping documents the seller is reimbursed by the bank. (*See also* Confirmed irrevocable letter of credit and Irrevocable letter of credit.)

Liabilities   All claims against a business. Liabilities include (a) accounts and wages payable; (b) taxes payable; (c) fixed and long-term liabilities (e.g. mortgage bonds, debentures and bank loans).

Licence   An arrangement whereby a business is permitted to do something which is otherwise forbidden (e.g. copy a product in return for a fee).

Lien   A right of possession on goods or property.

Life insurance   It was originally an arrangement for buying cover against the risk of death during a specific period of time. Nowadays it is also a means of saving over a long period and protecting purchasing power against erosion by inflation.

Liquidation   The winding up of a business. It may be voluntary or compulsory.

Liquidity ratio   *See* Quick ratio.

Loan   A sum of money lent with (and occasionally without) interest for an agreed term.

Loan capital   Money lent to a business on which interest is not determined by profits.

London Gazette   The publication which notifies changes in the status of companies.

Loss adjuster   A person or firm employed by an insurer to investigate the extent of liability following the submission of a claim under a specific policy of insurance.

Loss assessor   A person or firm employed by the insured to negotiate a claim.

Mail payment or **transfer**   Money sent by post from a foreign bank to a UK bank by post in a pre-arranged currency. The term also applies to money sent from a UK bank to a foreign bank by post.

Management by exception   The practice of directing attention to significant deviations between the actual and planned situation.

Management by objectives   Setting out the functions and responsibilities of executives with the aim of ensuring economic achievement of tasks and the maximization of profits.

Management buy-in   The purchase by members of management of a share of the business.

Management buy-out   The purchase of a business by the existing managers.

Mandate   A document authorizing a bank to open an account in the name of a business.

Marginal costing   *See* Direct costing.

Marine insurance   Insurance concerned with the carriage of goods and passengers by ships, vehicles and aircraft. The carriage of goods is sometimes known as *marine cargo insurance.*

Marketability   The ease or difficulty with which a share can be bought and sold.

Market maker   A securities dealer who is a principal and not an agent. They were formerly known as *jobbers.*

Members' voluntary liquidation   A solvent company wishing to cease trading prepares a declaration that its assets are greater than its liabilities and that its debts can be paid within twelve months and that it resolves to go into liquidation.

Merchant bank   An institution which provides finance on a large scale for foreign trade, management buy-outs and buy-ins, organizes public share issues, discounts and negotiates documentary credits.

Merger   An amalgamation of two or more businesses in which no one business is dominant (otherwise it would be a takeover).

Middle rate   The average of the buying and selling rates for a currency.

Minority interests   Shareholders who do not have a controlling interest. In another context the term refers to *consolidated accounts.*

Monetary items   Assets, liabilities or capital, the amounts of which are fixed by contract or statute in terms of the number of pounds irrespective of changes in the purchasing value of the pound.

Money market   The institutions which buy and sell currency and in so doing determine rates of exchange for one currency relative to another.

Money   In the context of this book, cash, *promissory notes* and other *negotiable instruments* (qv).

Mortgage   The conveyance of property by a debtor (mortgager) to a creditor (mortgagee) as security for a debt with the proviso that it shall be reconveyed on payment of the debt within an agreed period of time.

Mortgage debenture   A bond secured by a mortgage on property. The value of the property does not necessarily equal the value of the bonds issued against it.

Negotiable instrument   A document (e.g. bill of exchange, promissory note, cheque) which has a monetary value and may be transferred to another party for a consideration.

Net present value   A method of calculating and evaluating a project's expected returns. Future cash flows are discounted at a pre-determined rate (the cost of the capital) and their summation is then matched against the mutual capital expenditure.

Net worth   Total assets less total liabilities. Both issued shares and reserves are included. It is also known as *Total Shareholders' Interest*.

Nominal price   A price given by a market maker as an indication only of the market price. The market maker may not be prepared to deal at that price.

Nominal value   This term is also known as *par value*. It means the face value of a share.

Nominee shareholder   Someone who registers shares on behalf of a beneficial owner.

Non-absorption costing   The practice of changing all variable costs to the related operations, products or processes whilst changing indirect costs (i.e. overheads) to the income period in which they arise.

Non-convertible currency   A foreign currency which is not traded on the money market so it cannot be exchanged.

Non-monetary items   All items which are not monetary

items (i.e. share capital, reserves and retained profits). The total equity interest in a company is neither a monetary nor a non-monetary item.

Noting and protest A procedure when a bill of exchange is not accepted when presented.

Not negotiable A slightly misleading term because the document can still be negotiated. However the person or business taking the document cannot legally obtain a better title to it than the person or business from whom it was taken.

Not transferable A document which cannot be transferred to a third party (e.g. a cheque specified 'A/C payee only').

Obsolescence The ending of an asset's useful life.

Offshore (1) A company whose registered office is not in the British Isles.

(2) Investments outside the British Isles.

Open account A simple agreement, not without considerable risks, whereby the buyer promises to pay for goods after they are received.

Open cheque An uncrossed cheque which need not be paid into a bank account unlike a crossed cheque.

Open forward contract *See* Forward contract.

Open policy A term used for marine insurance purposes when the value of the goods is not known precisely.

Opportunity cost The benefits and gains foregone when the next most profitable use for the efforts of a business are not undertaken. For example the potential gains lost by not engaging in Activity B (the next best alternative) must be considered as part of the costs of engaging in Activity A.

Option The right to buy or sell at an agreed price at a future date.

Ordinary share A share or risk capital of a company.

Overdraft *See* Bank overdraft.

Overhead cost The total indirect cost of materials, wages, salaries and expense costs of the business.

Overtrading Doing more business than the working capital allows.

Par value *See* Nominal value.

Partnership Two or more people involved in the ownership of a business.

Payback The time taken to repay the initial cash outlays involved in capital investment.

Paying in book   A book issued by a clearing bank to a person or business in which details of cash and cheques paid into an account are recorded.

Pecuniary loss   *See* Business interruption.

Penny shares   Shares usually priced at less than 50p.

Penalty clause   A clause in a contract to the effect that a sum of money will be paid by the supplier in the event of late delivery.

Period cost   A cost which belongs to, and aggregates as a result of, a particular period of time and which tends to be unaffected by fluctuations in the levels of activity.

Petty cash   Money kept on business premises for the payment of small items of expense.

Placing   Shares sold to investors immediately prior to the start of dealings in a company new to the stock market.

Policy   (1) A course of action.

(2) A document relating to a contract of insurance or assurance.

Portfolio   A group of investments.

Preferential debts   If a company is wound up secured debts (i.e., preferential ones) have preference over unsecured ones.

Preference share   A class of share which has a claim on a company's earnings at a specified rate before payment to the ordinary shareholders if the company is liquidated. Cumulative preference shares have a provision that if one or more dividends is omitted the omitted dividend must be paid before dividends are paid on the company's ordinary shares.

Premium   The opposite of discount. (1) The extent to which a share price is above the issue or asset value price of a share.

(2) The payment on an insurance or assurance policy.

(3) When a foreign currency is more expensive to buy than at its normal exchange rate.

(4) A contractual arrangement to reward completion of work before an agreed target date.

Prepayment   A payment in advance.

Price Earnings ratio   The principal measure for evaluating a share. The share price is divided by earnings per share.

Price variance   The difference between the actual price and the standard price per item multiplied by the number of items purchased.

Prime cost   The total direct cost of materials, wages and expenses.

Process costing   A cost centre which consists of a continuous sequence of operations which are necessary to produce goods at the end of the operational service. It is normally used for high volume production. Total costs are divided by equivalent units of production output.

Product liability insurance   This type of insurance protects the insured against claims for injury to third parties, damage to property or its loss, brought about by goods supplied, repaired, sold, serviced or tested by the insured. The limit of indemnity is stated in the policy. The insured may incur a liability by way of common law, in negligence or in contract (e.g. Sale of Goods Act 1893).

Product mix   The varying mixture of products intended for sale which collectively make demands on the resources of a business.

Proforma invoice   (1) An invoice intimating that goods have been despatched usually by an overseas supplier but no payment is expected from the recipient other than customs duties in the receiving country.

(2) A demand for payment before goods are despatched.

Progress payment   An arrangement, usually associated with capital projects, whereby payments are made when previously agreed stages of work have been completed.

Promissory note   An unconditional promise in writing made by one person or business to another signed by the maker (i.e. customer engaging to pay on demand or at a fixed or determinate future time a sum certain in money to, or to the order of a specified person or business or to the bearer). They are used where suppliers and customers have a good relationship. Notes for large amounts may be discounted by acceptance houses and money made available via banks before the customer pays.

Proprietorship   An unincorporated business with a single owner.

Provision   An amount written off or retained by way of providing for (a) Depreciation, renewals or diminution in the value of assets; (b) A known liability which cannot be determined with substantial accuracy.

Public liability insurance   Insurance designed to cover claims made by members of the public for accidents caused by the actions attributable to the business, its personnel and activities.

Qualified acceptance   The acceptance of a bill of exchange which varies the effect of a bill as drawn.

Quantity variance   The difference between the actual quantity used and the standard quantity specified for the output actually produced multiplied by the standard price per item.

Quick ratio   The same as the *current ratio* except that stock is not included in the assets. *See also* Acid test.

Rate of exchange   The rate at which a foreign currency may be converted into another currency when buying or selling. Exchange commission is excluded.

Receiver   A person appointed to administer the property of a bankrupt.

Recourse   The right to proceed in connection with a documentary credit (e.g. bill of exchange). There are two categories: with and without recourse.

Refinancing   Credits obtainable by a foreign buyer where the exporter cannot provide credit and the buyer does not wish to pay cash.

Register of charges   All the charges on the property of a company: mortgages, fixed and floating charges/debentures, bills of sale.

Reinsurance   The practice of an insurer 'spreading' risk by reinsuring part of it with other insurers.

Renting back   An arrangement similar to *leaseback*. A business which has sold an asset rents it from the new owner and continues to use the asset.

Replacement cost   The cost of replacing an asset.

Replevin   The practice of restoring distrained goods to an owner.

Reserve gearing   Where a company has substantial reserves recorded in the total shareholders' interest then the issued preference shares and debentures are expressed in relationship with the issued ordinary shares plus the reserves and provisions.

Reserves   Funds which have been appropriated from after-tax profits and used for the purpose of increasing capital available for investing in fixed assets. Generally the growth in reserves shows the growth in wealth and represents a strengthening in the financial position of a business.

Retainer   A regular sum of money paid so that services may be available when required.

Retention   The money retained at the end of a large contract until it has been demonstrated that the supplier has satisfied the terms of the contract.

Return on capital   Pre-tax profit as a percentage of capital employed. As both capital employed and profit are terms without universally acceptable definitions, the value of this ratio as a measure of performance attracts criticism – although it is widely used.

Revaluation of assets   The practice of valuing assets of a business to bring them into line with current practices.

Revocable credit   Credit given by a banker willing to accept bills of exchange up to a certain value. The credit it revocable at any time without notice.

Revolving loan   A loan which varies in amount and possibly termination date.

Romalpa clause   The name originates from the decision of the court of appeal in the case of Aluminium Industrie Vaassen BV *v* Romalpa Aluminium (1976) Ltd. A supplier of goods may specify that the title to any goods physically passed to a purchaser remains with the supplier until certain conditions have been fulfilled by the purchaser (i.e. payment for the goods). If goods have been sold on by the purchaser to a third party or incorporated in equipment which cannot easily be dismantled, recovery of goods sold subject to a Romalpa clause may not be possible.

Royalty   A sum of money paid for the right to use the property of a tangible or intangible business for productive purposes.

Scrip issue   A free issue of shares to shareholders.

Secondary offering   An offer of shares by a quoted company to investors who need not necessarily be existing shareholders.

Secured creditor   A creditor whose debt is secured (e.g. by a charge on the property of the debtor).

Security   A general term for stocks and shares of all types.

Seed capital   Small loans and grants made to help start a business.

Self-liquidation   An asset the original cost of which is paid for out of earnings.

Semi-variable cost   A cost which is partly fixed and partly variable (e.g. telephone and electricity charges).

Service contract   A document setting out the length of service and terms of service (salary commission, pension) of a senior person.

Settlement day   The day on which bargains in securities must be paid for.

Shadow director   Excepting professional advisers, a person in accordance with whose directions or instructions the directors are accustomed to act, i.e., the 'power behind the throne'.

Share   A part proprietorship in an incorporated business.

Share premium   The amount paid in excess of a face value when a company sells shares.

Short bill   A *bill of exchange* payable on demand, at sight or within a shorter than usual period of time (e.g. 10 days).

Sight draft   Another name for a *bill of exchange* payable at sight (i.e., when it is presented).

Sinking fund   Money regularly set aside by a business to redeem its loan stock or preference shares from time to time. A sinking fund may also be used to make provision for the replacement of fixed assets.

Spot   A foreign exchange transaction which is settled two working days from the date of the deal (i.e., the majority of transactions).

Spread   The difference between a dealer's buying rate and the selling rate for a currency.

Spreadsheet   A computer program with financial planning uses, provided a personal or other computer with a large enough memory is available. Rows and columns of information are grouped into cells. The information in those cells may be manipulated and displayed on the monitor screen or VDU. The information may comprise a mixture of numbers, text and formulae. Provided the relationships between the different cells have previously been expressed as formulae (e.g. material = 0.45 labour costs) entering a new value in one cell causes all the values in interdependent cells to be recalculated.

Standard costing   A predetermined cost based on an expected (budgeted) attainable level of operations.

Standing order   An instruction to a bank to make regular, usually monthly payments, of a fixed amount.

Stock appreciation   The increase in the money costs of a given volume of stockholding.

Stock Exchange   A place where qualifying stocks and shares (securities) are bought and sold.

Stock profits   A term describing the consequences of rising replacement costs of stocks which enables a business to increase the selling price of its products immediately although it bought them at a price lower than the one subsequently prevailing.

Stock valuation   The value of stock for accounting purposes.

Strike price   *See* Exercise price.

Sunk cost   A cost which has already been incurred and which is irrelevant to any current or future decision.

Surplus   The excess of assets over liabilities and issued shares. When the surplus is accumulated from profits it is called 'retained earnings' and may be known (in part) as a general reserve. If it is from other sources it is called 'capital surplus'. The sale of shares at prices above the nominal value results in a premium equal to the excess of sale price over nominal value. The premium is shown in the balance sheet as a 'share premium account' (a form of capital surplus).

Surrender value   An assurance term for the amount a person or business will receive if a policy is cashed before it matures.

Swap   The purchase/or sale of currency in the spot market combined with a simultaneous purchase or sale in the forward market.

SWIFT   An electronic system for transferring money overseas: Society for Worldwide Interbank Telecommunications.

Takeover   The acquisition of the majority of shares in a company.

Tangible asset   Those assets of a company which can be seen and touched (e.g. plant, machinery, stocks).

Tax avoidance   A legitimate use of taxation provisions and legislation to achieve the maximum benefit for the taxpayer.

Tax evasion   The illicit concealment of data with a view to defrauding the taxation authorities.

Tax planning   The practice of organizing taxable activities and income to achieve the most beneficial result.

Telegraphic transfer   The use of telephone lines to move away from one bank to another, usually in connection with overseas transactions.

Tenor   A term used in connection with *bills of exchange* to indicate the time allowed between the date of drawing and the date of payment.

Term insurance   This is also known as *key person insurance*. It is cover on the life of a person (a) without whose services the business would be seriously disadvantaged, or (b) who has given personal guarantees or pledged other collateral as security. No payment is made if the insured person survives.

Term loan   A loan involving a fixed amount for a fixed time.

Third market   A stock exchange facility for companies which do not meet the requirements of a full listing or the unlisted securities market (e.g. small companies).

Time cost   A cost which exists and aggregates as a result of the passage of time and which tends to be unaffected by fluctuations in levels of activity.

Tranche   The sections into which large loans are divided for distribution to achieve a spread among financial institutions.

Traveller's cheque   A form of *bank draft* (i.e., it is paid for at the time of issue). Various currencies and cheque denominations are available.

Trustee   The nominal owner of property to be used for another's benefit.

Turnover of capital employed   The ratio of sales to capital employed.

Uncleared balance   Money paid into the bank of the receiver but not yet cleared by the payer's bank.

Uncontrollable cost   A cost which is not regulated or influenced by any action at a given level of managerial authority.

Underwriter   (1) A firm which guarantees to accept shares not taken up in an offer.

(2) A member of a Lloyds syndicate or individual employed by an insurance company who determines the risks to seek or avoid, fixed terms in the light of the specific hazards presented, stipulates the conditions or warranties to improve or maintain the risk at an acceptable level and executes an insurance policy.

Unit trust   An organization for the collective purchase and management of a range of shares which are then divided into units. The price of each unit is a precise fraction of the up-to-date value of the portfolio.

Unencumbered   Free of all charges. For example, property which is not mortgaged is said to be unencumbered.

Unsecured creditor   A creditor whose debts are not secured. In the event of a company being wound up they rank after secured creditors.

Updating   The process of translating figures of an earlier accounting period into current terms.

Usage variance   The difference between the actual quantity of material used and the pre-determined standard quantity multiplied by the number of goods produced.

Value added   The monetary increment added at each stage of manufacture.

Value date   The date at which delivery and date is due to settle a transaction.

Variable cost   A cost which tends to vary in the same proportion as variations in output.

Venture capital   Funds supplied for the launching or development of an ostensibly attractive product or business but with which there is an above average element of risk and on the other hand the possibility of an above average reward in the event of success.

Voluntary arrangement   A procedure whereby a business can come to terms with its creditors.

Warranty   An addition to a contract which releases the purchaser from the contract if the goods are unsatisfactory.

Working capital   The difference between current assets and current liabilities.

Work in progress   Work begun but not completed.

Writ   A legal document requiring a person to attend at a specified time and place and/or to perform a specified act.

Wrongful trading   Carrying on trading when there is no reasonable prospect that the company would avoid going into insolvent liquidation.

Yield   Also known as a *return*. The dividends or interest paid by a company expressed as a percentage of the current market price of the shares or debentures involved.

Z score   A collection of weighted ratios for credit control.

The pass mark is 3.0. Businesses most likely to fail score less than 1.8.

Part Five   Appendices

Appendix 1 Financial management and accounting computer programs

There are a number of computer programs available commercially which help the manager in the preparation of various essential financial records and with basic financial management calculations.

Records with audit trails
  Nominal ledger
  Purchase ledger
  Cash book
  Stocks
  Work in progress
  Asset register
  Bank statements

Document preparation
  Payroll
  Invoices
  Remittance advices
  Cheques

Reports
  Balance sheet
  Profit and loss account
  Trial balance
  Aged debts
  Sales analysis
  Purchase analysis
  VAT analysis
  Budget and actual comparisons

Forward projections using spreadsheets
  Budgets and financial forecasts

Calculations
  Discounted cash flow
  Compound interest
  Redemption yields
  Break even points
  Mortgage repayments
  APR (annual percentage rate) for loans and hire purchase

Programs designed for larger businesses are excluded from this list.

Appendix 2 World currencies

Alternative names are in brackets

Afghanistan	Afghani
Algeria	Algerian Dollar (Dinar)
Albania	Lek
Andorra	Franch Franc or Spanish Peseta
Angola	Kwanza
Argentina	Austral
Australia	Australian Dollar
Austria	Schilling
Bahamas	US Dollar
Bahrain	Bahrain Dinar
Bangladesh	Taka
Belgium	Belgian Franc
Bermuda	US Dollar
Bolivia	Bolivian Peso (Boliviano)
Botswana	Pula
Brazil	Cruzado
Brunei	Brunei Dollar
Bulgaria	Lev
Burma	Kyat
Canada	Canadian Dollar
Chile	Chilean Peso
China	Renminbi (Yuan)
Colombia	Colombian Peso
Congo	African Franc
Costa Rica	Colon
Cyprus	Cypriot Pound
Czechoslovakia	Kuruna
Denmark	Danish Krone
Dominican Republic	Dominican Peso
ECU (not a country)	European Currency Unit

Ecuador	Sucre
Egypt	Egyptian Pound
Ethiopia	Birr
Finland	Markka
France	French Franc
Gambia	Dalasi
East Germany	(Ost) Mark
West Germany	Deutsche Mark
Ghana	Cedi
Gibraltar	UK Pound
Greece	Drachma
Holland	Guilder (Florin)
Hong Kong	Hong Kong Dollar
Hungary	Forint
Iceland	Icelandic Krona
India	Indian Rupee
Indonesia	Rupiah
Iran	Iranian Rial
Iraq	Iraqi Dinar
Ireland	Irish Pound (Punt)
Israel	New Shekel
Italy	Italian Lira
Japan	Yen
Jordan	Jordanian Dinar
Kenya	Kenyan Shilling
South Korea	Won
Kuwait	Kuwaiti Dinar
Libya	Libyan Dinar
Liechtenstein	Swiss Franc
Luxembourg	Luxembourg Franc
Malawi	Malawi Kwacha
Malaysia	Malaysian Dollar (Ringgit)
Malta	Maltese Pound
Mexico	Mexican Peso
Morocco	Moroccan Dirham
New Zealand	New Zealand Dollar
Nigeria	Naira
Norway	Norwegian Krone
Oman	Omani Rial
Pakistan	Pakistan Rupee
Peru	Inti

Philippines	Filipino Peso
Poland	Zloty
Portugal	Escudo
Qatar	Qatar Rial
Romania	Leu
Saudi Arabia	Saudi Arabian Rial
Sierra Leone	Leone
Singapore	Singapore Dollar (Ringgit)
South Africa	Rand
Spain	Peseta
Sri Lanka	Sri Lankan Rupee
Sudan	Sudanese Pound
Sweden	Swedish Krona
Switzerland	Swiss Franc
Syria	Syrian Pound
Swaziland	Lilangeni
Taiwan	Taiwanese Dollar
Tanzania	Tanzanian Shilling
Thailand	Baht
Tunisia	Tunisian Dinar
Turkey	Turkish Lira
Uganda	Ugandan New Shilling
Uruguay	Uruguayan Peso
United Arab Emirates	United Arab Emirates Dirham
United States of America	US Dollar
USSR	Rouble
Yemen	Yemeni Rial
Yugoslavia	Yugoslavian Dinar
Zaire	Zaire
Zambia	Zambian Kwacha
Zimbabwe	Zimbabwe Dollar

Appendix 3 Abbreviations

Abbreviations are extensively used in business. Many managers of small businesses encounter abbreviations infrequently so they do not have the opportunity to familiarize themselves with their meanings because the practice is to dispense with indications of meanings. This list provides a source of reference to them when they encounter abbreviations.

When the abbreviations refers to a professional institute or association there is a single letter prefix indicating the grade of membership. (A Associate; M Member; F Fellow). The requirements for admission to these institutes and associations vary greatly in difficulty, as does movement from one category of membership to a higher one.

AAT	Association of Accounting Technicians
ABI	Association of British Insurers
ACT	Advance corporation tax
AFBD	Association of Futures Brokers and Dealers
ANOVA	Analysis of variance
APP	Appropriate personal pensions
APR	Annual percentage rates (for loans, charge cards and hire purchase payments)
ASC	Accounting Standards Committee
ARD	Accounting reference date
ATM	Automated teller machine
AVA	Auctioneers and Valuers Association
AVC	Additional voluntary contribution (pensions)
AWB	Airway bill
BE	Bill of exchange
BES	Business expansion scheme
BIIBA	British Insurance and Investment Brokers' Association

BL	Bill of lading
BTEC	Business and Technician Education Council
BOOT	Build own operate transfer
CAR	Compounded annual rate (of interest on deposits)
CAD	Cash against documents
CBI	Confederation of British Industry
CCA	Chartered Association of Certified and Corporate Accountants
CGT	Capital gains tax
CHAPS	Clearing House Automated Payments System
CIB	Chartered Institute of Bankers (*See also* CIOB)
CIFAS	Credit Industry Fraud Avoidance System
CIF	Cost insurance freight
CIFC	Cost insurance freight commission
CII	Chartered Institute of Insurers
CIMA	Chartered Institute of Management Accountants
CIMPS	Contracted Income Purchase Scheme (Pensions)
CIOB	Chartered Institute of Bankers
CIP	Freight, carriage and insurance paid to a named destination
CIPFA	Chartered Institute of Public Finance and Accountancy
C & F	Cost and freight (export prices)
COD	Cash on delivery
CONCISE	Containerized Cargo Insurance Service
CPP	Current purchasing power
CTCA	Consumer Trade Credit Association
CTT	Capital transfer tax
CV	(1) Corporate venturing (a form of cooperation between large and small companies). (2) Curriculum vitae
COV	Certificate of origin and value
DAA	Document against acceptance (of bill of exchange)
DCF	Discounted cash flow
DDP	Delivered duty paid
DCP	Freight carriage paid to a named carrier

DP	Documents against payment (of sight draft)
ECGD	Exports Credits Guarantee Department
EFEC	European Financial Engineering Company
EFTPOS	Electronic funds transfer at the point of sale
EIB	European Investment Bank
EIS	Executive information systems
EMS	European Monetary System
EPS	Earnings per share
ESOP	Employees share ownership plan
EVCA	European Venture Capital Association
FAR	Forwarding agents receipt
FAS	Free alongside ship
FCR	Forwarding certificate/receipt
FDD	Franc de droits. Free of charge (as when duty is paid in the country of shipment)
FECMA	Federation of European Credit Management Associations
FHA	Finance House Association
FIFO	First in first out (stock control)
FIMBRA	Financial Intermediaries Managers and Brokers Regulatory Organization
FOB	Free on board
FOQ	Free on quay
FOR	Free on rail
FOT	Free on truck
FRC	Free carrier
FSAVC	Free standing additional voluntary contribution (pensions)
HAWB	House air waybill (i.e., issued by a freight forwarder)
HOBS	Home and Office Banking Service
ICA	Institute of Chartered Accountants (see also ICAEW)
ICAEW	Institute of Chartered Accountants of England and Wales
ICC	International Chamber of Commerce
ICM	Institute of Credit Management
ICOF	Institute of Common Ownership Finance
IHT	Inheritance tax

IMRO	Investment Management Regulatory Organization
IPA	Insolvency Practitioners' Association
JIT	Just in time (a production control system with financial implications)
LAUTRO	Life Insurance and Unit Trust Regulatory Organization
LC	Letter of credit
LGS	Life guarantee scheme
LIA	Life Insurance Assessors
LIBOR	London Interbank Offered Rate
LIFE	London International Futures Exchange
LIFO	Last in first out (stock control)
MBA	Master of Business Administration
MBI	Management buy-in
MBO	Management buy-out
MIB	Motor Insurance Bureau
NHI	National Health Insurance
NIFO	Next in first out
OTC	Over the counter market
OFT	Office of Fair Trading
PAYE	Pay as you earn (tax)
PE	Price earnings ratio
PEP	Personal equity plan
PHI	Permanent health insurance
PIN	Personal identification number (cash cards)
PLN	Penalty liability notice (VAT offence)
POD	Proof of delivery
PRP	Profit related pay
RICS	Royal Institute of Chartered Surveyors
ROCE	Return on capital employed
SAYE	Save as you earn
SEAQ	Stock Exchange Automated Quotation System
SERPS	States Earnings Related Pension Scheme
SIB	Securities and Investment Board
SRO	Self Regulatory Organization

SSAP	Statements of Sources and Applications of Funds
SSP	Statutory sick pay
STAN	Standard cost
SWIFT	Society for Worldwide Interbank Financial Telecommunications
TAPS	Transcontinental Automated Payments Service (high volumes of small amounts)
UCITS	Undertakings for Collective Investment in Transferable Securities
UCP	Uniform customs and practice for documentary credits. (A brochure published by the ICC containing a universally accepted set of rules governing letters/credit.)
USM	Unlisted securities market

Appendix 4   Discounting tables

Table 1

Present value of £1 (what £1 due in the future is worth today)
$(1 + r)^{-n}$

Year	1%	2%	3%	4%	5%	6%	7%
1	0.9901	0.9804	0.9709	0.9615	0.9524	0.9434	0.9346
2	0.9803	0.9612	0.9426	0.9246	0.9070	0.8900	0.8734
3	0.9706	0.9423	0.9151	0.8890	0.8638	0.8396	0.8163
4	0.9610	0.9238	0.8885	0.8548	0.8227	0.7921	0.7629
5	0.9515	0.9057	0.8626	0.8219	0.7835	0.7473	0.7130
6	0.9420	0.8880	0.8375	0.7903	0.7462	0.7050	0.6663
7	0.9327	0.8706	0.8131	0.7599	0.7107	0.6651	0.6227
8	0.9235	0.8535	0.7894	0.7307	0.6768	0.6274	0.5820
9	0.9143	0.8368	0.7664	0.7026	0.6446	0.5919	0.5439
10	0.9053	0.8203	0.7441	0.6756	0.6139	0.5584	0.5083
11	0.8963	0.8043	0.7224	0.6496	0.5847	0.5268	0.4751
12	0.8874	0.7885	0.7014	0.6246	0.5568	0.4970	0.4440
13	0.8787	0.7730	0.6810	0.6006	0.5303	0.4688	0.4150
14	0.8700	0.7579	0.6611	0.5775	0.5051	0.4423	0.3878
15	0.8613	0.7430	0.6419	0.5553	0.4810	0.4173	0.3624
16	0.8528	0.7284	0.6232	0.5339	0.4581	0.3936	0.3387
17	0.8444	0.7142	0.6060	0.5134	0.4363	0.3714	0.3166
18	0.8360	0.7002	0.5874	0.4936	0.4155	0.3503	0.2959
19	0.8277	0.6864	0.5703	0.4746	0.3957	0.3305	0.2765
20	0.8195	0.6730	0.5537	0.4564	0.3769	0.3118	0.2584
21	0.8114	0.6598	0.5375	0.4388	0.3589	0.2942	0.2415
22	0.8034	0.6468	0.5219	0.4220	0.3419	0.2775	0.2257
23	0.7954	0.6342	0.5067	0.4057	0.3256	0.2618	0.2109
24	0.7876	0.6217	0.4919	0.3901	0.3101	0.2470	0.1971
25	0.7798	0.6095	0.4776	0.3751	0.2953	0.2330	0.1842
26	0.7721	0.5976	0.4637	0.3607	0.2812	0.2198	0.1722
27	0.7644	0.5859	0.4502	0.3468	0.2678	0.2074	0.1609
28	0.7568	0.5744	0.4371	0.3335	0.2551	0.1956	0.1504
29	0.7493	0.5631	0.4243	0.3207	0.2429	0.1846	0.1406
30	0.7419	0.5521	0.4120	0.3083	0.2314	0.1741	0.1314
40	0.6717	0.4529	0.3066	0.2083	0.1420	0.0972	0.0668
50	0.6080	0.3715	0.2281	0.1407	0.0872	0.0543	0.0039

$(1 + r)^{-n}$

Year	8%	9%	10%	12%	14%	15%	16%
1	0.9259	0.9174	0.9091	0.8929	0.8772	0.8696	0.8621
2	0.8573	0.8417	0.8264	0.7972	0.7695	0.7561	0.7432
3	0.7938	0.7722	0.7513	0.7118	0.6750	0.6575	0.6407
4	0.7350	0.7084	0.6830	0.6355	0.5921	0.5718	0.5523
5	0.6806	0.6499	0.6209	0.5674	0.5194	0.4972	0.4761
6	0.6303	0.5963	0.5645	0.5066	0.4556	0.4323	0.4104
7	0.5835	0.5470	0.5132	0.4523	0.3996	0.3759	0.3538
8	0.5403	0.5019	0.4665	0.4039	0.3506	0.3269	0.3050
9	0.5002	0.4604	0.4241	0.3606	0.3075	0.2843	0.2630
10	0.4632	0.4224	0.3855	0.3220	0.2697	0.2472	0.2267
11	0.4289	0.3875	0.3505	0.2875	0.2366	0.2149	0.1954
12	0.3971	0.3555	0.3186	0.2567	0.2076	0.1869	0.1685
13	0.3677	0.3262	0.2897	0.2292	0.1821	0.1625	0.1452
14	0.3405	0.2992	0.2633	0.2046	0.1597	0.1413	0.1252
15	0.3152	0.2745	0.2394	0.1827	0.1401	0.1229	0.1079
16	0.2919	0.2519	0.2176	0.1631	0.1229	0.1069	0.0930
17	0.2703	0.2311	0.1978	0.1456	0.1078	0.0929	0.0802
18	0.2502	0.2120	0.1799	0.1300	0.0946	0.0808	0.0691
19	0.2317	0.1945	0.1635	0.1161	0.0829	0.0703	0.0596
20	0.2145	0.1784	0.1486	0.1037	0.0728	0.0611	0.0514
21	0.1987	0.1637	0.1351	0.0926	0.0638	0.0531	0.0443
22	0.1839	0.1502	0.1228	0.0826	0.0560	0.0462	0.0382
23	0.1703	0.1378	0.1117	0.0738	0.0491	0.0402	0.0329
24	0.1577	0.1264	0.1015	0.0659	0.0431	0.0349	0.0284
25	0.1460	0.1160	0.0923	0.0588	0.0378	0.0304	0.0245
26	0.1352	0.1064	0.0839	0.0525	0.0331	0.0264	0.0211
27	0.1252	0.0976	0.0763	0.0469	0.0291	0.0230	0.0182
28	0.1159	0.0895	0.0693	0.0419	0.0255	0.0200	0.0157
29	0.1073	0.0822	0.0630	0.0374	0.0224	0.0174	0.0135
30	0.0944	0.0754	0.0573	0.0334	0.0196	0.0151	0.0116
40	0.0460	0.0318	0.0221	0.0107	0.0053	0.0037	0.0026
50	0.0213	0.0184	0.0085	0.0035	0.0014	0.0009	0.0006

$(1 + r)^{-n}$

Year	18%	20%	22%	24%	25%	26%	28%
1	0.8475	0.8333	0.8197	0.8065	0.8000	0.7937	0.7813
2	0.7182	0.6944	0.6719	0.6504	0.6400	0.6299	0.6104
3	0.6086	0.5787	0.5507	0.5245	0.5120	0.4999	0.4768
4	0.5158	0.4823	0.4514	0.4230	0.4096	0.3968	0.3725
5	0.4371	0.4019	0.3700	0.3411	0.3277	0.3149	0.2910
6	0.3704	0.3349	0.3033	0.2751	0.2621	0.2499	0.2274
7	0.3139	0.2791	0.2486	0.2218	0.2097	0.1983	0.1776
8	0.2660	0.2326	0.2038	0.1789	0.1678	0.1574	0.1388
9	0.2255	0.1938	0.1670	0.1443	0.1342	0.1249	0.1084
10	0.1911	0.1615	0.1369	0.1164	0.1074	0.0992	0.0847
11	0.1619	0.1346	0.1122	0.0938	0.0859	0.0787	0.0662
12	0.1372	0.1122	0.0920	0.0757	0.0687	0.0625	0.0517
13	0.1163	0.0935	0.0754	0.0610	0.0550	0.0496	0.0404
14	0.0985	0.0779	0.0618	0.0492	0.0440	0.0393	0.0316
15	0.0835	0.0649	0.0507	0.0397	0.0352	0.0312	0.0247
16	0.0708	0.0541	0.0415	0.0320	0.0281	0.0248	0.0193
17	0.0600	0.0451	0.0340	0.0258	0.0225	0.0197	0.0150
18	0.0508	0.0376	0.0279	0.0208	0.0180	0.0156	0.0118
19	0.0431	0.0313	0.0229	0.0168	0.0144	0.0124	0.0092
20	0.0365	0.0261	0.0187	0.0135	0.0115	0.0098	0.0072
21	0.0309	0.0217	0.0154	0.0109	0.0092	0.0078	0.0056
22	0.0262	0.0181	0.0126	0.0088	0.0074	0.0062	0.0044
23	0.0222	0.0151	0.0103	0.0071	0.0059	0.0049	0.0034
24	0.0188	0.0126	0.0084	0.0057	0.0047	0.0039	0.0027
25	0.0160	0.0105	0.0069	0.0046	0.0038	0.0031	0.0021
26	0.0135	0.0087	0.0057	0.0037	0.0030	0.0025	0.0016
27	0.0115	0.0073	0.0047	0.0030	0.0024	0.0019	0.0013
28	0.0097	0.0061	0.0038	0.0024	0.0019	0.0015	0.0010
29	0.0082	0.0051	0.0031	0.0020	0.0015	0.0012	0.0008
30	0.0070	0.0042	0.0026	0.0016	0.0012	0.0010	0.0006
40	0.0013	0.0007	0.0004	0.0002	0.0001		
50	0.0003	0.0001					

$(1 + r)^{-n}$

Year	30%	35%	40%	45%	50%
1	0.7692	0.7407	0.7143	0.6897	0.6667
2	0.5917	0.5487	0.5102	0.4756	0.4444
3	0.4552	0.4064	0.3644	0.3280	0.2963
4	0.3501	0.3011	0.2603	0.2262	0.1975
5	0.2693	0.2230	0.1859	0.1560	0.1317
6	0.2072	0.1652	0.1328	0.1076	0.0878
7	0.1594	0.1224	0.0949	0.0742	0.0585
8	0.1226	0.0906	0.0678	0.0512	0.0390
9	0.0943	0.0671	0.0484	0.0353	0.0260
10	0.0725	0.0497	0.0346	0.0243	0.0173
11	0.0558	0.0368	0.0247	0.0168	0.0116
12	0.0429	0.0273	0.0176	0.0116	0.0077
13	0.0330	0.0202	0.0126	0.0080	0.0051
14	0.0254	0.0150	0.0090	0.0055	0.0034
15	0.0195	0.0111	0.0064	0.0038	0.0023
16	0.0150	0.0082	0.0046	0.0026	0.0015
17	0.0116	0.0061	0.0033	0.0018	0.0010
18	0.0089	0.0045	0.0023	0.0012	0.0007
19	0.0068	0.0033	0.0017	0.0009	0.0005
20	0.0053	0.0025	0.0012	0.0006	0.0003
21	0.0040	0.0018	0.0009	0.0004	0.0002
22	0.0031	0.0014	0.0006	0.0003	0.0001
23	0.0024	0.0010	0.0004	0.0002	
24	0.0018	0.0007	0.0003	0.0001	
25	0.0014	0.0006	0.0002		
26	0.0011	0.0004	0.0002		
27	0.0008	0.0003	0.0001		
28	0.0006	0.0002			
29	0.0005	0.0002			
30	0.0004	0.0001			
40					
50					

Table 2

Present value of £1 per year (what £1 receivable annually is worth today)

$$\frac{1 - (1 + r)^{-n}}{r}$$

Year	1%	2%	3%	4%	5%
1	0.9901	0.9804	0.9709	0.9615	0.9524
2	1.9704	1.9416	1.9135	1.8861	1.8594
3	2.9410	2.8839	2.8286	2.7751	2.7232
4	3.9020	3.8077	3.7171	3.6299	3.5460
5	4.8534	4.7135	4.5797	4.4518	4.3295
6	5.7955	5.6014	5.4172	5.2421	5.0757
7	6.7282	6.4720	6.2303	6.0021	5.7864
8	7.6517	7.3255	7.0197	6.7327	6.4632
9	8.5660	8.1622	7.7861	7.4353	7.1078
10	9.4713	8.9826	8.5302	8.1109	7.7217
11	10.3676	9.7869	9.2526	8.7605	8.3064
12	11.2551	10.5753	9.9540	9.3851	8.8633
13	12.1337	11.3484	10.6350	9.9856	9.3936
14	13.0037	12.1062	11.2961	10.5631	9.8986
15	13.8651	12.8493	11.9379	11.1184	10.3797
16	14.7179	13.5777	12.5611	11.6523	10.8378
17	15.5623	14.2919	13.1661	12.1657	11.2741
18	16.3983	14.9920	13.7535	12.6593	11.6896
19	17.2260	15.6785	14.3238	13.1339	12.0853
20	18.0456	16.3514	14.8775	13.5903	12.4622
21	18.8570	17.0112	15.4150	14.0292	12.8212
22	19.6604	17.6580	15.9369	14.4511	13.1630
23	20.4558	18.2922	16.4436	14.8568	13.4886
24	21.2434	18.9139	16.9355	15.2470	13.7986
25	22.0232	19.5235	17.4131	15.6221	14.0939
26	22.7952	20.1210	17.8768	15.9838	14.3752
27	23.5596	20.7069	18.3270	16.3296	14.6430
28	24.3164	21.2813	18.7641	16.6631	14.8981
29	25.0658	21.8444	19.1885	16.9837	15.1411
30	25.8077	22.3965	19.6004	17.2920	15.3725
40	32.8347	27.3555	23.1148	19.7928	17.1591
50	39.1961	41.4236	25.7298	21.4822	18.2559

$$\frac{1 - (1 + r)^{-n}}{r}$$

Year	6%	7%	8%	9%	10%
1	0.9434	0.9346	0.9259	0.9174	0.9091
2	1.8334	1.8080	1.7833	1.7591	1.7355
3	2.6730	2.6243	2.5771	2.5313	2.4869
4	3.4651	3.3872	3.3121	3.2397	3.1699
5	4.2124	4.1002	3.9927	3.8897	3.7908
6	4.9173	4.7665	4.6229	4.4959	4.3553
7	5.5824	5.3893	5.2064	5.0330	4.8684
8	6.2098	5.9713	5.7466	5.5348	5.3349
9	6.8071	6.5152	6.2469	5.9952	5.7590
10	7.3601	7.0236	6.7101	6.4177	6.1466
11	7.8869	7.4987	7.1390	6.8052	6.4951
12	8.3838	7.9427	7.5361	7.1607	6.8137
13	8.8527	8.3577	7.9038	7.4869	7.1034
14	9.2950	8.7455	8.2442	7.7862	7.3667
15	9.7122	9.1079	8.5595	8.0607	7.6061
16	10.1059	9.4466	8.8514	8.3126	7.8237
17	10.4773	9.7632	9.1216	8.5436	8.0216
18	10.8276	10.0591	9.3719	8.7556	8.2014
19	11.1581	10.3356	9.6036	8.9501	8.3649
20	11.4699	10.5940	9.8181	9.1285	8.5136
21	11.7641	10.8355	10.0168	9.2922	8.6487
22	12.0416	11.0612	10.2007	9.4424	8.7715
23	12.3034	11.2722	10.3711	9.5802	8.8832
24	12.5504	11.4693	10.5288	9.7066	8.9847
25	12.7834	11.6536	10.6748	9.8226	9.0770
26	13.0032	11.8258	10.8100	9.9290	9.1609
27	13.2105	11.9867	10.9352	10.0266	9.2372
28	13.4062	12.1371	11.0511	10.1161	9.3066
29	13.5907	12.2777	11.1584	10.1983	9.3696
30	13.7648	12.4090	11.2578	10.2737	9.4269
40	15.0463	11.3317	11.9246	10.7574	9.7791
50	15.7619	13.8007	12.2335	10.9617	9.9148

$$\frac{1 - (1 + r)^{-n}}{r}$$

Year	12%	14%	15%	16%	18%
1	0.8929	0.8722	0.8696	0.8621	0.8475
2	1.6901	1.6497	1.6257	1.6052	1.5656
3	2.4018	2.3216	2.2832	2.2459	2.1743
4	3.0373	2.9137	2.8550	2.7982	2.6901
5	3.6048	3.4331	3.3522	3.2743	3.1272
6	4.1114	3.8887	3.7845	3.6847	3.4976
7	4.5638	4.2883	4.1604	4.0386	3.8115
8	4.9676	4.6389	4.4873	4.3436	4.0776
9	5.3282	4.9464	4.7716	4.6065	4.3030
10	5.6502	5.2161	5.0188	4.8332	4.4941
11	5.9377	5.4527	5.2337	5.0286	4.6560
12	6.1944	5.6603	5.4206	5.1971	4.7932
13	5.4235	5.8424	5.5832	5.3423	4.9095
14	6.6282	6.0021	5.7245	5.4675	5.0081
15	6.8109	6.1422	5.8474	5.5755	5.0916
16	6.9740	6.2651	5.9542	5.6685	5.1624
17	7.1196	6.3729	6.0472	5.7487	5.2223
18	7.2497	6.4674	6.1280	5.8178	5.2732
19	7.3658	6.5504	6.1982	5.8775	5.3162
20	7.4694	6.6231	6.2593	5.9288	5.3527
21	7.5620	6.6870	6.3125	5.9731	5.3837
22	7.6446	6.7429	6.3587	6.0113	5.4099
23	7.7184	6.7921	6.3988	6.0442	5.4321
24	7.7843	6.8351	6.4338	6.0726	5.4509
25	7.8431	6.8729	6.4642	6.0971	5.4669
26	7.8957	6.9061	6.4906	6.1182	5.4804
27	7.9426	6.9352	5.5135	6.1364	5.4919
28	7.9844	6.9607	6.5335	6.1520	5.5016
29	8.0218	6.9830	6.5509	6.1656	5.5098
30	8.0552	7.0027	6.5660	6.1772	5.5168
40	8.2438	7.1050	6.6418	6.2335	5.5482
50	8.3045	7.1327	6.6605	6.2463	5.5541

$$\frac{1 - (1 + r)^{-n}}{r}$$

Year	20%	22%	24%	25%	26%	28%
1	0.8333	0.8197	0.8065	0.8000	0.7937	0.7813
2	1.5278	1.4915	1.4568	1.4400	1.4235	1.3916
3	2.1065	2.0422	1.9813	1.9520	1.9234	1.8684
4	2.5887	2.4936	2.4043	2.6346	2.3202	2.2410
5	2.9906	2.8636	2.7454	2.6893	2.6351	2.5320
6	3.3255	3.1669	3.0205	2.9514	2.8850	2.7594
7	3.6046	3.4155	3.2423	3.1611	3.0833	2.9370
8	3.8372	3.6193	3.4212	3.3289	3.2407	3.0758
9	4.0310	3.7863	3.5655	3.4631	3.3657	3.1842
10	4.1925	3.9232	3.6819	3.5705	3.4648	3.2689
11	4.3271	4.0354	3.7757	3.6564	3.5435	3.3351
12	4.4392	4.1274	3.8514	3.7251	3.6059	3.3868
13	4.5327	4.2028	3.9124	3.7801	3.6555	3.4272
14	4.6106	4.2646	3.9616	3.8241	3.6949	3.4587
15	4.6755	4.3152	4.0013	3.8593	3.7261	3.4834
16	4.7296	4.3567	4.0333	3.8874	3.7509	3.5026
17	4.7746	4.3908	4.0591	3.9099	3.7705	3.5177
18	4.8122	4.4187	4.0799	3.9279	3.7861	3.5294
19	4.8435	4.4415	4.0967	3.9424	3.7985	3.5386
20	4.8696	4.4603	4.1103	3.9539	3.8083	3.5458
21	4.8913	4.4756	4.1212	3.9631	3.8161	3.5514
22	4.9094	4.4882	4.1300	3.9705	3.8223	3.5558
23	4.9245	4.4985	4.1371	3.9764	3.8273	3.5592
24	4.9371	4.5070	4.1428	3.9811	3.8312	3.5619
25	4.9476	4.5139	4.1474	3.9849	3.8342	3.5640
26	4.9563	4.5196	4.1512	3.9879	3.8367	3.5656
27	4.9636	4.5243	4.1542	3.9903	3.8387	3.5669
28	4.9697	4.5281	4.1566	3.9923	3.8402	3.5679
29	4.9747	4.5312	4.1585	3.9938	3.8414	3.5687
30	4.9789	4.5338	4.1601	3.9951	3.8424	3.5693
40	4.9966	4.5439	4.1659	3.9995	3.8458	3.5712
50	4.9995	4.5452	4.1666	3.9999	3.8461	3.5714

$\dfrac{1 - (1 + r)^{-n}}{r}$

Year	30%	35%	40%	45%	50%
1	0.7692	0.7407	0.7143	0.6897	0.6667
2	1.3609	1.2894	1.2245	1.1653	1.1111
3	1.8161	1.6959	1.5889	1.4933	1.4074
4	2.1662	1.9969	1.8492	1.7195	1.6049
5	2.4356	2.2200	2.0352	1.8755	1.7366
6	2.6427	2.3852	2.1680	1.9831	1.8244
7	2.8021	2.5075	2.2628	2.0573	1.8829
8	2.9247	2.5982	2.3306	2.1085	1.9220
9	3.0190	2.6653	2.3790	2.1438	1.9480
10	3.0915	2.7150	2.4136	2.1681	1.9653
11	3.1473	2.7519	2.4383	2.1849	1.9769
12	3.1903	2.7792	2.4559	2.1965	1.9846
13	3.2233	2.7994	2.4685	2.2045	1.9897
14	3.2487	2.8144	2.4775	2.2100	1.9931
15	3.2682	2.8255	2.4839	2.2138	1.9954
16	3.2832	2.8337	2.4885	2.2164	1.9970
17	3.2948	2.8398	2.4918	2.2182	1.9980
18	3.3037	2.8443	2.4941	2.2195	1.9986
19	3.3105	2.8476	2.4958	2.2203	1.9991
20	3.3158	2.8501	2.4970	2.2209	1.9994
21	3.3198	2.8519	2.4979	2.2213	1.9996
22	3.3230	2.8533	2.4985	2.2216	1.9997
23	3.3254	2.8543	2.4989	2.2218	1.9998
24	3.3272	2.8550	2.4992	2.2219	1.9999
25	3.3286	2.8556	2.4994	2.2220	1.9999
26	3.3297	2.8560	2.4996	2.2221	1.9999
27	3.3305	2.8563	2.4997	2.2221	2.0000
28	3.3312	2.8565	2.4998	2.2222	2.0000
29	3.3317	2.8567	2.4999	2.2222	2.0000
30	3.3321	2.8568	2.4999	2.2222	2.0000
40	3.3332	2.8571	2.5000	2.2222	2.0000
50	3.3333	2.8571	2.5000	2.2222	2.0000

Index